HIKING THE BACKCOUNTRY

HIKING THE BACKCOUNTRY

A Do-It-Yourself Guide for the Adventurous Woman

Jackie Johnson Maughan
and
Ann Puddicombe

STACKPOLE BOOKS

Hiking the Backcountry
Copyright © 1981 by Jackie Johnson Maughan and Ann Puddicombe

Published by
STACKPOLE BOOKS
Cameron and Kelker Streets
P.O. Box 1831
Harrisburg, Pa. 17105

Published simultaneously in Don Mills, Ontario, Canada
by Thomas Nelson & Sons, Ltd.

Illustrations by Janis Rockwell
Cover photograph by Charles J. Farmer

Printed in the U.S.A.

Library of Congress Cataloging in Publication Data

Maughan, Jacqueline Johnson, 1948–
   Hiking the backcountry.

   Bibliography: p.
   Includes index.
   1. Backpacking.   2. Outdoor recreation for women.
I. Puddicombe, Ann, 1946–   joint author.   II. Title.
GV199.6.M38   1981   796.5′1   80-27095
ISBN 0-8117-2170-1

Dedication

To Ralph B. Maughan and George Matejko

Contents

Preface

THIS BOOK IS designed not only to encourage women to enter the backcountry, but to give credit where credit is due. Women are increasing their field of endeavors, and the wilderness is yet another arena. Most of the writing about the wilderness experience is still done primarily by men. Men, understandably, put more emphasis upon themselves. They may be concerned about women, but surely not as much as women are.

This book is for women who want to acquire or sharpen outdoors skills. It is a means of providing information that applies directly to women. We want to acknowledge women's skills and contributions. We think women are tired of being relegated to the recipe columns of *Field and Stream*. We believe that women want to watch a Canadian Honker wing southward through the September mist, rather than just cook one.

We have included personal stories, anecdotes and information gathered from women and men all over the United States and some foreign countries. Massive hours of research were devoted to make the book as accurate as possible. We know that women are capable of digesting complex information and fully suspect that they are anxious to learn more about themselves.

Much of the information included in the book was gathered from women by means of a detailed questionnaire. Many women were interviewed personally. In all, the results are an accumulation of experience which extends well beyond what we, as authors, can personally claim.

Ann Puddicombe is a woman with extensive backcountry experience. She is now a public information officer for the United States Forest Service. I am a conservationist who does a lot of backpacking and presently on the board of directors of the Idaho Conservation League and the Idaho Environmental Council.

We believe that the "future lies ahead," as the comic Shelley Berman once quipped.

However, joking aside, it's up to women to make the most of it. Hopefully, this book will be a catalyst to do just that.

JACKIE JOHNSON MAUGHAN

Acknowledgments

AMONG THOSE WHO were kind enough to share their time and expertise with us, are many who agree with the spirit of the book. However, the inclusion of their names here does not indicate that their opinions and ours are the same.

Myrna Ahlgren, public information technician, Ranier, Minnesota; Virginia Bailey, teacher, Lake Fork, Idaho; Melinda Bowler, wilderness instructor, Pocatello, Idaho; Katherine Bridwell-Bos, law student, Sacramento, California; Janice M. Brown, field advisor, Idaho Falls, Idaho; Kathryn A. Bulinski, range conservationist, Redding, California; Linda C. Burke, crew leader, Youth Conservation Corps, McCall, Idaho; Beverly Cochrane, guide and writer, Greenville, Maine; Cynthia Copeland, wilderness coordinator, Butte, Montana; Julia Corbett, writer-editor, Idaho Falls, Idaho; Hillary Dustin, range conservationist, Dunlap, California; Joyce Lee English, graduate student, Pocatello, Idaho; Kellie Erwin, outdoor instructor, Pocatello, Idaho; Jo Ellen Force, college professor, Pullman, Washington; Linda Furtado, administrative secretary, Orinda, California; Flora Goldstein, hydrolic technician, Shoshone, Idaho; Mary Griffith, community organizer, Brunswick, Maine; Mary Grisco, counselor and educator, Pocatello, Idaho; Christine B. Hastedt, bus driver, teacher's aid, clam digger, Freeport, Maine; Melissa B. Holsten, homemaker, Jackson, Wyoming; Liz Howard, civil engineering technician, St. Anthony, Idaho; Sara Johnson, wildlife biologist, St. Anthony, Idaho; Nada Skidmore Kovalik, secretary/treasurer, Wilderness World, Inc., Pacific Grove, California; Becky Lankford, student, Denver, Colorado; Jennifer Lee, administrator, educator, Concord, New Hampshire; Cynthia Marquette, conservationist, Fairbanks, Alaska; Pauline Miller, retired, McCall, Idaho; Shelia Mills, outfitter and boatperson, Pocatello, Idaho; Doris Milner, conservationist, Hamilton, Montana; Victoria Montgomery, civil engineering technician, Salmon, Idaho; Virginia Norris, businesswoman, Tetonia, Idaho; Molly O'Leary-Hudson, photographer, McCammon, Idaho; Eunice Olson, resource assistant, St. Anthony, Idaho; Virginia H. Puddicombe, homemaker, Santa Barbara, California; Mary Lou Reed, conservationist, Coeur d'Alene, Idaho; Norma Jean Sands, marine biologist, Krokelvadalen, Norway; Cindy Shott, secretary, Red Lodge, Montana; Cyndy Simer, mountaineering instructor, Lander, Wyoming; Linda Sturges, graphic artist, San Francisco, California; Nelle Tobias, conservationist, McCall, Idaho; Lindi Wall, expedition leader and driver, Cheshire, England; Karen Wells, homemaker, Idaho Falls, Idaho; Virginia Williams, teacher, Freeport, Maine; Julie Wind, Philomath, Oregon; and Marji "Slim" Woodruff, guide, Phoenix, Arizona.

In addition to those who answered the questionnaire are others who contributed substantially through advice, review, and correspondence. These include Ralph B. Maughan, political science professor, Pocatello, Idaho; Robert W. Puddicombe, engineer, Santa Barbara, California; Deanne Shulman, forestry technician, Santa Barbara, California; and Alex Urfer, parks and recreation management professor, Pocatello, Idaho.

Others who corresponded with us at some length or aided in other ways are Irene Ayres, mountaineer, Gainesville, Florida;

Irene Beardsley, mountaineer, Santa Barbara, California; Winona G. Campbell, M.D., mountaineer, Denver, Colorado; Beverly Cochrane, Allagash Canoe Trips, Greenville, Maine; Georgia Engelhard Cromwell, mountaineer, Unterseen, Switzerland; Merle Friedenberg, co-founder, Adventure Center, Oakland, California; Charles Houston, M.D., mountaineer, Burlington, Vermont; Polly Lankford, Lankford Mountain Guides, Denver, Colorado; Carol Alice Liska, mountaineer, Los Alamos, New Mexico; Luci Malin, range conservationist, Eugene, Oregon; Virginia E. Nolan, mountaineer, Denver, Colorado; Polly Prescott, mountaineer, Cleveland, Ohio; Margaret Prouty, M.D., mountaineer, Madison, Wisconsin; and Christine L. Reid, mountaineer, Cambridge, Massachusetts.

Others who should be mentioned are James Albert, Outback O'Maine, Clinton, Maine; Anna M. Alden, Osprey River Trips, Inc., Grants Pass, Oregon; Eleanore E. Bartlett, mountaineer, Greenbrae, California; Linda Gray Burdet, mountaineer, Lyndonville, Vermont; Cecily Clark, mountaineer, Ossipee, New Hampshire; Stella Degenhardt, mountaineer, Seattle, Washington; Eleanor D. Ehrman, mountaineer, Colorado Springs, Colorado; Peter H. Hackett, M.D., mountaineer, Denver, Colorado; Paul W. Horton, Jackson Hole Mountain Guides, Teton Village, Wyoming; Michael S. Kaye, Costa Rica Expeditions, San Jose, Costa Rica; Barbara King, Encounter Overland, San Francisco, California; Vera Komarkova, mountaineer, Boulder, Colorado; Darvel Lloyd, Keystone Environmental Center, Dillon, Colorado; Sandra Rider, South American Wilderness Adventures, Berkeley, California; Roy Smith, Challenge/Discovery, Crested Butte, Colorado; Sherry Spurlin, Nanthala Outdoor Center, Inc., Bryson City, North Carolina; Mike Wolters, wildlife biologist, Santa Ynez, California; and Art Woodworth, secretary/treasurer, Western River Guides Association, Inc., Salt Lake City, Utah.

1

The Outdoorswoman

EARLY LAST FALL, just after the autumnal equinox, my husband and I were hiking the gentle rolling backcountry of Yellowstone National Park. Nightfall was coming fast, and we knew we couldn't make it to the campsite the green clad ranger had designated for us when we registered with the United States Park Service.

We saw no one. Few people are on the trail that time of year, and fewer still are willing to step off the boardwalks of developed sites like Old Faithful for fear of ending up in the claws of a grizzly.

I count myself among those who are certain that bears hide behind the trees in the park impatiently waiting for innocent backpackers. But in a fit of bravado, one night in the safety of our living room, I'd challenged, "Why don't we ever hike the Yellowstone backcountry?" Previously we had never gotten past the sites depicted on calendars because I'd refused. Whenever he would unroll the topographic maps, I would inquire suspiciously about bear sightings in the area in question. Then I would remind him that official bear sightings only become so if confirmed by at least three wildlife biologists, all armed with doctorates of philosophy.

Even then, they like evidence, like a 28mm close-up, a plaster cast, or maybe the humped-trapezius bear itself. "For every 'official' sighting, there are probably fifty grizzlies rampaging around," I'd tell him.

So what was I doing here? Why had I let him drag me under threat of absolute and permanent loss of dignity into one of the most famous grizzly preserves in the world? I looked to the ranger for fortification and inquired mildly, "What about bears?" As my questions were evaded, the more strident I became. Finally, the ranger, secure in his cabin for the oncoming night, admitted there had indeed been grizzly sightings and trail closures in a very nearby area. I wished desperately that my husband would leave the room. If I could get that ranger alone, he'd tell the truth. Another backpacker stomped in. Another male. So much for allies. My husband delicately inquired of his trip and asked if he'd seen any "wildlife." Onto us, he answered blandly that he had seen a wolverine. "Nice time of year to hike," he commented. "Hardly any people." As we left I looked around for the rest of his party—no women in sight.

A half-hour to the trailhead, then the crossing of the Falls River. Curiously, my fear faded the further we got from the river, giving way to caution, which gave way to security. What bear in its right mind would be in here, I thought. Nothing to eat, nowhere to fish, and nothing but lava rock to scrape its tired feet on. However, caution made me methodically inspect our first campsite. Caution led me to discover a bear den dug under the gigantic root system of a fallen pine.

We hiked on rapidly for another mile or so, and he started navigating off the trail in a southward direction to get over the park boundary so we wouldn't be illegally camped. When we felt safe, we set up our new, blue, guy-line free, arch-bow supported tent and gathered firewood.

Night came quickly, and a howling wilderness descended upon us. The elk were in rut, and as the darkness deepened, they began to bugle—an undulating low-keyed bugle that rose to a high pitch and ended in a scream, then repeated and answered throughout the darkest hours. Then we heard stomps, scuffles, and branches breaking somewhere off in the night. The campfire light was the only thing between us and the howling beasts. When we went to hang our food in a tree for the night, we couldn't have hiked more than a few hundred yards into the blackness around us, however, it seemed like we crossed centuries back to the tree dwellers.

Outside of the circle of man-made fire, warmth, and security, I reflected that absolute wilderness is not an ideal state for humans, especially female humans. Primitive woman, her belly big with child and perhaps two little ones in tow, could not have felt completely safe or comfortable knowing that large carnivores visited the same berry patches as she and her young ones, or that the woods might hide a rapacious member of a hostile tribe. No, it wasn't all sweetness and natural food.

So why was I contrarily trying to recapture the very thing eons of forebears had tried to stamp out? To get back to nature? My mind recoiled at the cliché. Using the best gear that industry and civilization had to offer—Rip-stop, down parkas, Thinsulite, tempered steel Buck knife, plastic bags, and other assorted goodies—was not getting back to nature. But where else could I hear the wild carryings-on of the mating elk? Where else could I muse at the indignant little pikas darting among the rocks and scolding all the while? I liked knowing I was strong enough to hike for miles and shoulder a heavy pack. I liked the beauty the wilds had to offer. And I especially liked the religious cathedral-in-the-trees feeling of being close to creation. The blisters, sore

WAPITI – AMERICAN ELK

muscles, occasional fear, possible accidents, and the inconvenience of keeping dirt out of the dinner pot were things to be put up with, not an end in themselves.

My Yellowstone trip was hardly my first wilderness experience, but it was my first venture into overcoming a personal nemesis. In retrospect I scoff, sort of. The venture was hardly a major strike for women's equality because I wouldn't have been there if it weren't for my husband. I needed him for navigation and companionship. I was not the women who climbed Annapurna One with two dying on that frigid rib of the Himalayas. Nor was I Jennifer, who hiked the park without man, woman, or child to drive away the isolation and vulnerability. But I was on my way, and one victory leads to others.

Is the wilderness experience distinctly different for women than it is for men? Most men will immediately dismiss the idea. Many are antagonistic. But women find the idea intriguing. Actually, there are numerous differences between the sexes in terms of strengths and weaknesses, perceptions, roles, occupations, culture, and history. These forces aren't going to shut down once you leave the city.

Psychological Differences

In adjusting to the wilds, women are overcoming centuries of typecasting which has associated them with personal adornment, domesticity, the need to be protected, and introspective, circumspect life-styles. Conversely, males have been associated with the outdoors, activity, and adventure.

Some of the most important personality traits for outdoors recreation and professions are defined by our culture as healthy for men but unhealthy for women. Independence, objectivity, and adventurousness in women has often put them on the psychiatrist's couch. Many very successful outdoorswomen are accused of being overly competitive and "just trying to prove themselves." While this may be true, the same objection is rarely leveled against successful outdoorsmen. Often, it's that very need for admiration that puts people on that rock ledge or gets them to the summit.

This is not to say that women lack ambition or that all men will charge out on cliffs of rotten lava to prove their manhood.

Women are simply more likely to admit they're tired, cold, hungry, or scared, since doing so isn't a threat to their manhood. At the same time, while women tend to appraise their various skills and weaknesses more realistically, they may demand too little of themselves, especially when in the company of men who are accustomed to taking charge. This is best remedied by taking turns at decision making and leadership, or by going with women to eliminate the temptation to lean on a broad male shoulder.

In general, women are less likely to engage in unnecessary risks. Nor would they assume that one person should be stuck with KP while everyone else goes fishing. They are usually less interested in distance and scaling peaks than in having a good time. Many of the women surveyed echoed Katherine Bridwell-Bos, a former environmental consultant and range technician in California, who said, "We view the whole experience differently. Men are in a hurry to get someplace. Women take time to absorb their environment."

Sensory Differences

It is a much researched and documented superiority in women that they are more aware of subtle changes in their environment. (1) Women have better peripheral vision and constantly scan their surroundings while men will concentrate on what's ahead. Women also are better at noticing detail. As a result, they should be better at noticing game tucked away in the forest, while the men are searching earnestly for the creatures on the ridge looming ahead. From early childhood on, however, the male responds better to visual display and reacts to it quicker. His speed at getting out of the way of a charging moose may be quicker than yours.

Men are also more sensitive while in the light. This obscure bit of information coupled with the fact that they have better phototropic visual acuity means that they are better at focusing on both immobile and moving targets. If you hunt, a male has this advantage. He might not be a better hunter because numerous female skills are needed for this venture, such as awareness of surroundings, manual dexterity, an eye for detail (broken branches, tracks, movement) and enough empathy with the animal to figure out where it's going or what it might do next.

Even though she is more aware of her surroundings and has a better visual memory, a woman won't necessarily be able to navigate better. Many studies show that men have better depth perception and better spatial ability. (2) A male partner has this perceptual advantage when it comes to reading maps and being able to relate the lines to the actual lay of the land. It doesn't mean that women can't equal and excell men in this ability. It will just take them more effort to do so.

Because of her awareness of her environment, a woman will probably notice the minor changes in breeze, temperature, cloud buildup, and other signs of an approaching storm. Marji "Slim" Woodruff, a guide who has logged over 2,500 miles in the Grand Canyon, says that changes in weather bring to mind "my old bugaboo about climbing high peaks in the thunder season." Since the man is never supposed to show fear or concern, "it's up to me," she says, "to say I'm scared of lightning and I'm getting out of here. Then he'll come along ostensibly to keep me company." She also reports that experienced women get nervous at the same time she does and study the clouds just as anxiously when a storm begins to build. Of course, she notes, this is assuming that the women are experienced enough to recognize that they are indeed taking risks. If they don't know enough to realize they are in danger, it's not quite the same thing. Culturally, women are supposed to be dull, staid, and sensible when it comes to survival. But when common sense is called dull and staid, Slim says, our society has indeed become too competitive.

Many women have probably suffered guiltily from the accusation that they "see and hear" things at night while the men sleep on unperturbed. It could be that they are just spooked, or it could be that there *are* things out there that men aren't aware of. Women see better in the dark. (3) They also hear better. (4) Even while asleep, women are more aware of sound and more likely to respond to it. While this superior ability in sight and hearing may be a hassle when you're trying to get to sleep, don't think yourself a coward because you "hear" things. Once you become accustomed to what are normal and unthrea-

tening night sounds, you will be more at ease. Should a real
threat arise, you'll probably be the first to notice it.

Superior hearing is an asset for boaters since falls and rapids
are often heard before they're seen. Women are better than men
at locating a sound source. They are also more sensitive to
intensity and volume. Tolerance to sound is about 75 decibels
for women. Anything louder than that is painful. For men this
tolerance level is 83 decibels. Since loudness doubles in intensity to those who hear it at about 10 decibels, by the time the
level of 85 decibels is reached, it will seem twice as loud to
women. As a woman, you should be able to tell more accurately
how big that rapid or drop is going to be. This advantage can
be used to make up for your slower physical reaction time.

Women are usually light-years ahead of men in empathy.
Because of this some women would rather hike, climb, et cetera
solely with other women. In one study of newcomers entering
a play group (5), girls as young as three years responded to new
children with affection, interest, comforting actions, and talk.
The newcomers were initially ignored by the boys and excluded
from their games. Other studies show that males prefer objects
to people while females prefer people. Women are also more
compassionate. Bev Cochrane, co-owner of Allagash Canoe
Trips in Maine, observes that women have spent most of their
lives attuned to the needs of others. "While I'm not necessarily
an advocate of this one-sided situation, I think that as a result,
women are more responsive and more quickly aware of the
physical or emotional distress of novices in their care," she
says.

The fact that women are more sensitive in social situations
has led to the conclusion that they are also more sensitive physically, translating into the assumption that they register pain
quicker. A look at the research shows mixed results. In one
study, newborn females showed significantly higher responses
to pain and physical changes, such as removal of a covering
blanket. However, further research on sensitivity showed that
second and later children have greater sensitivity than firstborn
children, regardless of sex. "If the mechanism here is a physiological one, it is a very mysterious one indeed," the researcher
said. (6)

Women and girls may merely acknowledge pain faster than a man. One man tells of a hiking companion who wore new boots on an extended trip. After two hobbling days and fifteen miles, the friend's feet were blistered and bloody. The man hadn't admitted the mess his feet were in. Another male friend was miles into the wilderness before he acknowledged that he was in excruciating pain because he had started the trip with a cracked ankle bone. Although experienced women know that a little (and sometimes a lot) of stoicism is important when mountaineering, it's hard to imagine a woman being so stupidly heroic.

Complaining women are favorite targets in satire, and the theme of the ailing woman who holds up a party to the point of disaster is a fairly common one. However, the double-barreled factors are that since women are assumed, often correctly, to have less experience in the wilds than men, they are more likely to complain; and because women are assumed to be weaker, they are more likely to get hurt. However, there is no evidence to support the last contention. In fact, some evidence, which will be presented later, suggests just the opposite.

Many people also associate hysteria and panic with women. One woman, who is a lands specialist for the United States Bureau of Land Management in California, says she's been extremely disturbed by the overly emotional, off-the-handle reactions of women under stressful circumstances. At the scene of an accident, for example, they could have better expended their energy caring for some victim, but didn't have the training to "take themselves in hand."

Melinda Bowler, an outdoor education instructor in Idaho, speculates that because women are usually less experienced, in an unfamiliar environment, have fewer skills and strengths, and are therefore in a more dependent position in the wilderness, they therefore feel less responsibility. "Maybe they can afford the luxury of panic," she says. A man realizes his responsibility and thus cannot panic.

"On our trips," says one boater, "many more men than women have panicked. A total of four of them positively freaked out. Of the women who panicked, all did it very quietly."

Another guide comments that less experienced women might

tend to panic more easily than less experienced men. "I have seen women get hyper over a dog loose on the trail. But I've also seen a grown man sit up all night because I told him ring-tailed cats were in the area. He imagined a cougar-sized cat coming into camp to carry him off." She feels that men are not allowed by our society to panic, so they bottle it up inside when they are afraid.

"Panic is a reaction that indicates lack of experience or skill. It could as easily happen to men as women," sums up Janice M. Brown, a former field advisor for the Girl Scouts.

Physical Differences

It's sad but true that most men are more physically fit than most women. However, a deliberate and systematic effort coupled with role expectations have prevented women from developing their strength. Not until the last decade has a woman been atop any of the world's fifteen peaks of over 26,000 feet, while male teams had climbed most of these by the end of the 1950s. Women were not invited along as participants on the summit teams of these expeditions, nor did they expect to be. Women had to first expect to be able to make it to the top of the world's highest peaks before they would make such a demand or endeavor.

The women we surveyed, with a few exceptions, said they were not as strong as their male partners, could not carry as much weight and were slower. "I set the pace," many said, "because I'm slower." Of those who were as strong, some said that men are chagrined to learn that a woman can outpace them.

Early in life, boys are more active and exploratory than girls. As they grow, their speed and physical reaction time outstrips the girls. This ability parallels their muscular development. Interestingly, there are strong genetic components in how fast men can react and in their muscle power, while no such individual level has been identified in women. (7) This could well mean that strength in women has been developed so little that no one knows how fast we could react or strong we could be if given equal lifelong training and expectations.

While the average male is better at gross muscular response

and strength, women have more manual dexterity and are more sensitive to touch in their hands. Rock climbers report a difference in the way women approach a rock face than the way men do. Women usually feel their way up the rock, depending more on balance and precision for their progress. Men will more often clamber up the face relying on strength.

When speaking of gross muscle power, men do seem to be superior. This makes some men condescending and downright callous to women mountaineers, especially novices. "I was in a climbing class," says one woman. "Of the thirty women who enrolled, only eight finished. I think this was because the men climbed faster and were stronger. Most were very impatient with the women. On one occasion a man above was supposed to belay me. He got bored waiting, he said, and started chatting with another climber. Just then I lost my balance. I fell twenty feet before he got his wits together and caught hold of the rope I was attached to. I was mad as hell, as well as scraped all up and down my legs. He shrugged it off as my fault because I was 'taking too long.'"

Attitudes toward women have changed some since the time of the incident described (six years ago). Many men have slowed down enough to accommodate slower partners and allow newcomers to enjoy the trip. And many women are getting strong enough to make the trip more than just perpetual labor. Hopefully, women and men can meet somewhere in the middle. Although women, at least most women, are still not as strong as men of equal size and weight, they are capable of developing the strength and skills needed to explore the backcountry.

Strength is an inclusive, generic term, full of ambiguities and possibilities. When someone refers to strength, she may mean general health and well-being, endurance, muscle power, the ability to withstand environmental stress, the ability to work for long hours, self reliance, the ability to survive, or the ability to influence and manipulate one's circumstances.

When viewing strength as an overall concept, women have a number of strengths which men don't have and vice versa. A great deal of research has been done on this topic in recent years by almost every work/sports physiology research center in the world. One of the principals has been the United States

Air Force because the first United States women astronauts will soon enter space.

"This debate has been carried on much more keenly at times when the existing roles and statuses of males and females are changing," says Ann Oakley in her book *Sex, Gender and Society*. The debate emerged in the nineteenth century with the beginnings of the movement for emancipating women, she notes. However, even among these early feminists, many believed that nature dictated some sex differences whose social significance was obvious—bodily strength, for example, she says. Much of the new research, in addition to the increased activity of women in the outdoors and in athletics, has led to a reassessment of women's ability to handle adverse circumstances and "work." Those which are relevant to the wilderness experience will be dealt with separately.

Cold. Do women get cold faster than men? In exposure to mild cold, they do better because their higher fat content serves as insulation. In extreme cold, yes and no. Since women are generally smaller and have a greater surface-to-mass ratio (more skin surface in relation to body weight) than men, they can get cold faster. (8) Being small means they lose heat faster, much like a small pan of water cools faster than a large one. If you are exposed to extreme cold for long periods of time, it's harder for your body to maintain its inner (core) temperature. This is dangerous, since once you are cold through-and-through you're in danger of hypothermia. However, a woman's extra body fat helps offset this danger. Small and slender women should take special precautions to keep warm, while large and chunky women don't have to worry about other than normal precautions.

Small to average-sized women may be more likely to get frostbite, cold feet, cold hands, cold ears et cetera than larger persons. This is due to size, not sex. In spite of a lower skin temperature, a woman's extremities (when size is not a factor) are not more susceptible to cold injury. The lower female skin temperature is probably explained by greater beneath-the-skin fat deposits. (9)

Some inexperienced or inactive women will get cold faster

than healthier partners, female or male. The cold tends to bother a physically fit person less.

Heat. The average woman is less heat tolerant than the average man. Women working in heat have higher heart rates, and fainting is more common. However, in one study, a difference great enough to matter appeared only in the most severe, humid heat. (10)

In moderate heat, small people adjust and achieve thermal equilibrium better than larger people. In extreme heat, like in extreme cold, the woman's greater surface-to-mass ratio is a disadvantage because it allows rapid heat gain or loss. This is aggravated by being small, which, again like in extreme cold, means your body will heat up more easily.

Women working in heat have two other potential disadvantages. One is that at all times they have a higher heart rate. This could be to compensate for the fact that their blood doesn't carry as much oxygen as a man's, so their hearts pump faster to get more oxygen to the cells. Women also have more skin per pound for the blood to get to. The greater surface-to-mass ratio means what blood there is has more skin to keep cool. What this all seems to add up to is that women's hearts may have to work harder to adjust their bodies to the heat and that more blood rushes to the skin and away from the core of the body to cool the skin. This could account for why women are more likely to faint.

Women also do not sweat as much as men. This advantage has been foolishly cited as a reason why women can't work in hot environments. It was assumed that a lot of sweat was a sure sign of health. It's now well accepted that a lot of sweating just leads to greater water loss. Some researchers (11) praise the economy of the female sweat control, describing the male as a "prolific and wasteful sweater." Another study showed that heat increased the metabolic requirements of men more than women (12), so men need to eat and drink more.

Traditional life-styles account for the fact that the average woman does not do as well, in the desert for example, as the average man. "Women are conventionally exempt from labor in hot conditions and avoid the physical training which in men is associated with partial heat acclimatization," relates Dr. Sarah A. Nunneley, United States Air Force School of Aerospace Medicine. Multiple reports indicate that women can adjust to heat successfully, in about the same time and way that men do. "The women in these studies did not achieve the highest levels of heat tolerance observed in men," she says, "but each experiment covered only a short period of time and involved women with low work capacities."

In sum, women seem to have the same problems adjusting to heat as they do to cold and for similar reasons. Extremes in either are a problem for the small, slender woman. The other disadvantages can be overcome or compensated for with physical fitness. Yes, she probably will have to work harder, but it can be done.

Oxygen. Women do not use oxygen as efficiently as men. They have fewer red blood cells per unit of blood than men. It is the red blood cells that carry the oxygen to the muscle cells. Coupled with this obstacle is that even with training, the number and size of energy-producing oxygen converters in the muscle cells do not increase as much in women as in men who train similarly. (13)

A woman's greater percentage of body fat is another negative factor along with her lower percentage of muscle. Because all conversion of oxygen for energy use takes place in the muscle cells, a woman's greater percentage of body fat is a negative factor.

Altitude. In some ways it appears that women adjust more readily to altitude than men while in other ways it seems they do not.

In one study (14) women overcame the loss of appetite often associated with exposure to altitude more quickly than did the men. After one week women ate the same as they would at lower altitudes while the men ate less than normal even at the end of two weeks. In these studies the weight loss in men was 4.86 percent, while in women it was 1.49 percent after a two week period.

In another method of altitude adjustment (altitude acclimatization) the body is thought to adjust to the thinner air by more rapid and deeper breathing, termed hyperventilating. In the same study, women hyperventilated at high altitude to a greater degree than men. The researcher noted that a young British woman, Mable Purefoy FitzGerald, pioneered research in this area as a member of the Anglo-American expedition to Pikes Peak seventy-five years ago. His studies confirmed FitzGerald's findings and showed that women increased ventilation by 18 percent after twelve hours while it took men about two days to do the same.

A third way that these studies showed a female advantage was that in the women studied, the number of red blood cells increased per unit of blood by almost double that in men while at high altitude. This is identified as hemoconcentration and is yet another way the body adjusts to the lack of oxygen in the air at high altitudes. However, when looking at the results of this study it is important to remember that in all situations, low and high altitude, women do not have as many red blood cells per unit of blood as men. This ability to hemoconcentrate may be only a compensation for the lower ability of a woman's blood to carry oxygen in the first place.

In another set of studies there was evidence that women are more likely to develop peripheral edema (fluid retention) at high altitude than men. (15). In this study 15 percent of the female trekkers measured near Mt. Everest had edema in more than one area (such as the hands, face, and feet).

Peripheral edema by itself is not particular cause for worry. However, its presence is cause for concern since it may lead to more serious complications such as pulmonary edema. In pulmonary edema the air sacs of the lungs fill with fluid and block off air.

The researchers also reported a predominance of retinal hemorrhage in women. Retinal hemorrhages, which can result in defects in vision which can be permanent, seem to occur rather commonly at high altitudes. The researcher commented that of the eight women who suffered from retinal hemorrhage, none were taking birth control pills, not a minor point because some medical doctors do feel that birth control pills may increase the hazards associated with high altitudes. The researcher noted that the amount of time taken to adjust to high altitudes is a very important factor and that some of the women who suffered from retinal hemorrhages had flown rather than walked in to the Himalayan area thereby increasing their susceptibility to acute mountain sickness.

In another study in which the same researcher participated during the fall of 1979, one hundred trekkers were measured. "In that study in which our definition of acute mountain sickness was more stringent, we found that there was a twenty-one percent incidence in women (eight out of thirty-eight), and only a fourteen percent incidence in men (eight out of fifty-nine). When this is worked out statistically, the difference is only marginally significant, he commented. "I think that the bottom line, as of 1980, is that there has not been proven any statistically significant difference in incidence of acute mountain sickness between men and women," he said.

The studies discussed do not necessarily contradict each other. It is entirely possible that women show different maladjustments to altitude than men. It is also possible that their adaptation to altitude may take place in a somewhat different manner.

Endurance. Both biology and psychology favor women when strength means the ability to survive the brutality of hardship and starvation.

Biology makes it so women in general live longer, are less prone to disease, and don't require as much food. Women have a lower metabolic rate, consequently a woman does not require as much food to accomplish the same tasks as a man of similar height, age, and weight. Men use five more calories per pound to maintain themselves than women. (16) Although this fact has put women on a perpetual diet in cultures where food is abundant, the irony is that it makes her a superior survivor. Her greater body fat content is also a plus because her body will live off its fat before it starts to metabolize its muscle (meat). Although men have more muscle power, women seem to have more muscle endurance, (17)

Psychology also favors women since they are less aggressive, more cautious and less likely to put themselves in a survival situation to begin with.

These points are dramatically illustrated by the story of the Donner Party. This pioneer expedition of over eighty persons was snowbound in California's Sierra Nevada Mountains during the winter of 1846. The disaster in which members of the party had to make the awful choice between cannabilism and starvation is the most spectacular in the records of the western migration across the United States.

The Donner Party consisted of 16 women, 31 men, 18 girls, and 22 boys. Of these 66 percent of the women survived, 72 percent of the girls, 45 percent of the boys, and 33 percent of the men.

Author George R. Stewart, writing in his book *Ordeal by Hunger*, said "About this time they must have begun to notice what afterwards seemed to them so astonishing. The women stood the strain better than the men did. Whether the food was apportioned by individuals rather than by size, whether the men did more physical work and therefore expended more energy, whether the constitution of a woman is more enduring than that of a man, whether merely in these individual cases the women were hardier—these questions cannot be surely answered. Most likely several of these factors were at work, but certainly, with some exceptions, the men failed sooner." (18)

It is hard to know how food was apportioned, but it is probable that the women didn't eat more than their share. Given the cultural background of self-sacrifice, it seems fair to suppose that the women may have given some of their food to their husbands and children. In Stewart's account, with one exception, in the only instances in which food was voluntarily given to another person or family, it was the women who did the giving. In one family, against the knowledge and wishes of her husband, the wife kept another family's starving child alive by sneaking food to her.

Since there were only 16 women to care for 41 children, many of whom were infants, it is unfair to speculate that the women did less work. This is an oversight of definition where only chopping wood and hunting are defined as work. It does appear that men did most of the woodcutting. But in the course of the three-month ordeal, only a couple of birds, one bear, and one deer where ever brought in by hunters. There was precious little game since the party was encamped well above winter pasture.

It is also unlikely that the individual women were hardier than the men. One-third of the women were over 35-years-old, while only 23 percent of the men were. Of the men who did not survive, one-half were under 35. Only one woman under the age of 35 died.

Although it was men who led the various rescue attempts, the women did not sit passively in camp and let the men take all the risks. Every survivor of the Donner Party got out on her or his own power; including the children, except one or two who were carried part of the way. All the members of the party lived through blizzards, frostbite, and starvation. All either walked out or died.

The first group to cross what is now named the Donner Pass, best illustrates the survival capacity of women. Unaided by a rescue party, the group consisted of five women and twelve men, representing those who deemed themselves strong enough to make the crossing. It took them 33 days to climb over the mountains. They suffered starvation, blizzards, and resorted to cannibalism. Only eight survived, all five women but only three men.

Psychologically, the Donner women did seem better suited for survival than their men. No women picked fights or died in them, nor did they kill another human being. Some of the men did.

What became of many of the male survivors is unknown. Many were single and caught up in the westward expansion. However, since all but one of the Donner women were part of family groups and hence more stable, history does have a record of them. It seems that all of the female survivors went on to live relatively happy and productive lives. The family grouping may well have given its members a social and psychological edge, although the death toll among single men was not particularly greater than their married counterparts.

Most of the historical, biological, and psychological evidence points to the conclusion that men have greater immediate strength, while women do better in the long run in backcountry activities. This consistency has led to a search for a biochemical explanation. Whatever it is that seems to be at work appears so early in life that many think it takes place in the womb before the child is born.

Why is it that most men in most cultures are larger and more muscular than women? Why are male infants more active than female infants? Why is it that men have institutionalized aggression such as war and women rarely participate in physical attack? Why do men seem better suited for the kill be it in warfare or the hunt? Why are men more likely to risk their lives without logically weighing the consequences before doing so?

In looking for the biological answer, many researchers have come to regard the sex hormones as a possible explanation. Bodily differences between the sexes such as height, weight, and muscle composition are not the complete answer since culture can have a profound influence on them. For example, in western societies the daughter of a professional worker is likely to be as tall as the son of an unskilled worker.

The general group of male hormones known as androgens and the female hormones of estrogen and progesterone occur in both sexes. However, normal women usually have a greater amount of female sex hormones, and normal men have more male hormones.

At puberty, the increase in growth of both sexes is caused by an increase in the production of androgens. But in girls the rise in estrogen levels causes the bones to mature and stop growing. (19) Because teenage boys have low levels of estrogen in their bodies, they have a longer time to grow before their bones mature. In western societies boy babies are about an inch longer at birth than girls and weigh slightly more. There is also some evidence that the genes located on the X (female) chromosome may inhibit the development of large muscles.

Another curious fact is that the male sex hormone is related to the sexual drive in both women and men. If a man has his testes removed, it threatens his sex drive. Not so with removal of a woman's ovaries. When women are given male hormones during medical treatment, they produce a striking increase not only in sexual desire but in activity and aggression. (20)

Androgens also effect muscular strength and energy by influencing the use of nitrogen in the body. Nitrogen, taken by the body from protein, is needed for growth, red cell volume, and blood plasma. With fewer androgens, women may not use nitrogen as well. This could account for their lower red blood cell count, plasma volume, and bodily growth.

In the famous studies by Dr. John Money, two men he treated for a lack of androgens reported a substantial increase in their fatigue thresholds after treatment. Two women treated by Money for an excess of male hormones reported a parallel decline in muscle strength and energy after the treatment to reduce their level of male hormones. (21)

Are androgens responsible for aggression? Animals from chickens to mice, to gerbils, to the rhesus monkey have been loaded with androgens or castrated to eliminate the androgens to see how they would behave. In most cases, increased androgens "caused" increased aggression, and decreased androgens "caused" decreased aggression. Social situations can alter the levels of male hormones in the body. In animals as well as man, learned behavior can override the effects of hormones. (22)

The question of whether or not men are more aggressive than women because of hormones becomes even more interesting when linked with the primitive lower brain centers which are thought to produce the rage or "go" response in humans and animals. Some speculate that one of the lower brain centers is especially sensitive to androgen and that it also inhibits the production of the hormone prolactin which is most closely associated with maternal behavior. By linking the two—androgens and this lower brain center (the amygdala)—some people might conclude that men are not only more likely to be aggressive because of their hormones but that this lower brain center working with the androgens triggers the rage response. (23) It is also possible that due to these factors, women and men actually perceive things differently. Where he sees a threat, she doesn't. When a child aims a snowball at their car, he sees an aggressor, while she notices that the child has no mittens on and worries over its cold hands.

If all of this is true, it happens in the womb and predisposes the person to indelible sex-typed behavior. However, all of this is still speculation or as one writer put it, "not yet compelling." (24)

Separating out the influences of culture on aggression is extremely difficult. The social setting may bring out and encourage the biology at work. If we assume that people can choose how they behave, then men apparently choose to be more aggressive. Regardless, looking both at organized aggression such as war and individual aggression such as violent crime, men lead the the field.

How this carries over into wilderness situations is much the same as the impact it has on life in the city. Men lead, women follow. Men hunt, women don't. Women are more compassionate toward animals than men are. Women are attacked by men in the backcountry. Men are attacked by men in the backcountry. Women don't often attack anything, animal or human. Women rarely carry firearms in the wilderness, while for men the hunt is a major reason for being there.

While aggression is basically a negative impulse, that can ruin a trip or put people in unnecessary danger, it is still something a woman may have to use to defend herself. Maintaining your own dignity and rights without harming others is the obvious answer for both sexes. If you tell other people what you think rather than just smoldering in anger then everyone can conspire to make decisions for the happiness and comfort of all.

2

Equipment

TO ENJOY YOUR backcountry experience, it is important to have the right gear. All outdoors people worry about weight, and for most women this is a major consideration. Lightweight items cost more than others. If you aren't in a hurry, wait for sales. Cooperatives that sell mountaineering gear are cheaper than other mountaineering sales outlets.

Although the theory of unobtrusive tents, packs, and other gear is beginning to gain ground, it is impractical. Brightly colored tents and accessories are easier to locate. It's nice to see that flash of blue through the trees indicating that camp has been found. A red parka will make a partner easier to see, particularly if she's lost and hurt or unconscious. A yellow canoe will be a lot more visible than a brown or gray one. And if a tent occupies a campsight one's been counting on, its color won't matter a great deal. A brown tent takes just as much space as a red or blue one.

Gear

Backpacks

Next to boots, this is probably your most important purchase both in cost and comfort. The main items to look for in a pack are 1) type of material, 2) how well it is put together, 3) size, 4) amount of storage, arrangement space, and compartments, 5) comfort (especially in shoulder and waist straps), 6) weight, and 7) waterproofing.

There are three basic types of packs: a rigid-frame pack which has a lightweight aluminum outer support; a variation of the rigid-frame manufactured by Alpinlite which has a wrap-around frame and allows the hips to move independently of the shoulders and places most of the weight on them; and internal-frame packs with a flexible-metal inner support system that can be molded to your body. Some backpackers argue that the rigid-frame is the only one that will provide proper support and adequate carrying capacity. An added feature of the Alpinlite frame is that it can stand independently without being propped against a tree. Others feel that the inner-frame works just as well and won't get caught on branches and other extrusions (a small point on the surface, but one which one observer says just may have saved his life). Since internal-frame packs press against your body; they tend to cause you to sweat more.

Do not let your boyfriend, husband, trail boss, or supervisor stick you with an "army" style pack (a pack without a frame and straps without padding) because they don't want to buy you a good pack until they are sure you will like backpacking. Many men complain that women don't like backpacking. If they had to hike with makeshift equipment, they wouldn't be sold on backpacking either. A bargain backpack is usually built for schoolchildren to carry their lunches in, not serious outdoor use. Insist on adequate equipment.

Backpacks can be borrowed. However, the borrower should be choosy and still look for a comfortable pack with all the qualities previously mentioned. Some backpack stores rent packs with the option to buy.

On long trips, a small, lightweight, waterproof day pack is good to use for short jaunts. This way you can carry all your essentials—food, water, compass, fishing gear—while you explore. These need not be expensive and can be obtained from most sporting goods stores. When stored in the big pack, the day pack can serve as a container for food and clothing. At night, when you must hang your food, the day pack can serve as a food bag. It can also be stuffed with excess clothes and used as a pillow.

The common backpacking rule is to carry no more than one-third your own weight, however it is more comfortable with only one-quarter your weight. Try to stick to this lower weight during your first backpack trip. This weight rule is hard on small people during long trips since they have to be especially conservative about what they take with them.

Backpacks come in small, medium, large, and extra large sizes. If you are a small woman, a small pack that fits you probably won't have enough carrying capacity for more than a three-day trip. Some small women travel with a small-sized rigid frame to which they attach a large or medium-sized pack. Kletterwerks has a small-frame body pack and Trailwise has a small frame rigid pack that still have large carrying capacities.

Before going on a long hike, some people fill their backpacks with rocks or other heavy items to become accustomed to the long haul. This is also a very good practice when purchasing a pack. A retailer should be willing to allow you to try on the pack with weights (often sandbags) to get the feel of it.

Since most men have more upper body strength than women, they can carry more weight on their shoulders. For this reason, you may want a pack that distributes more of the weight on the waist strap. Among these are the Alpinlite and the JanSport D–3. The JanSport D–3 has a removable waist suspension bar. Many packs have an attachment for a sleeping bag on the lower part of the frame. Since a sleeping bag will weigh between four to six pounds and therefore is your heaviest item outside of a tent, this type of pack is preferable for most women.

A strap with good padding is a necessity. This is true of the shoulder and waist straps. When you fit your pack, make sure it rides just above your pelvic bone, not right on it. Women's pelvic bones protrude more than men's and consequently will

INTERNAL FRAME

JANSPORT D-3
RIGID FRAME PACK

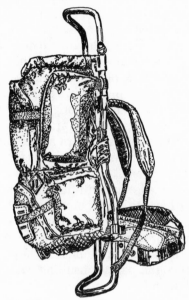

ALPENLITE
RIGID FRAME PACK

register pain if there is a strap rubbing against them. Should this situation occur, tie a sweatshirt or jacket underneath for extra padding. Bra strap attachments are occasionally rubbed by shoulder straps. Practice before the big hike to see if this will present you with a problem.

The army-style pack is great for people with no nerve endings in their shoulders. The straps cut sharply into the shoulder blades, can cause neck and back pain, and can deaden your upper body. If your arms go to sleep, even in a good pack, check the straps and readjust them. Walking along with your arms elevated once in awhile also helps. If your arms go to sleep in the early stages of your hike (the first mile or so) and adjusting the straps does not provide relief, you are probably carrying too much weight.

Since no pack has been made that will put all of the weight on your hips, you may have to rest more frequently due to shoulder pain than a male partner. Temporary relief can come from leaning against a tree or bending over while keeping your legs straight. Sometimes hooking your thumbs in the straps near the shoulder helps relieve the pain or bending over as far as practical when going downhill or uphill will help.

Although this is mainly a matter of personal preference, the number of outside pockets on a pack can mean a difference in time and convenience. Some people don't mind dumping the entire contents of their pack on the ground to find their toothbrushes. Whether you're of the "accountant" mentality or the "let-it-all-hang-out" school makes little difference as long as you buy a pack to suit your personality. The fewer pockets a pack has, the more material that can be devoted to carrying capacity. If you need to carry a lot, you may have to sacrifice on the pockets.

Accountant types like to know where everything is. It's easier to find your water bottle if it's in the same compartment each time. Snacks, knives, maps, and binoculars are more accessible if you have a few zippered nooks and crannies to store them in for quick accessibility on the outside. The let-it-all-hang-outers claim you don't save any time whatsoever with all that metal work since you have to take the pack off anyway to get to items and besides, that's just more zippers to break.

Whether your pack has outside pockets or not, it should be

tough, lightweight, and durable. The pack material should be strong, durable, and waterproof. Check the stitching and rivets to see if the thread is sturdy and/or double stitched and if the parts look and feel secure. A broken strap is a major calamity. Make sure that the shoulder, waist, and suspension straps are adjustable to account for differences in physique. This means money and comparison shopping but buying a good pack is worth it in the long run. You may soon be substituting bandanas for waist straps if you buy a cheap pack.

The basic concern in packing your pack is load distribution and convenience. Women generally feel most comfortable with the greatest weight at the bottom of the pack. Consequently, not only do they load their stoves and other heavy items at the bottom, but they also attach their sleeping bags to the bottom straps. This varies with the kind of pack you purchase. The best way to arrange items by weight is arrived at through trial and error. If you pack too much weight at the bottom, the top will flay out from your shoulders and cause the shoulder straps to bind.

Even those who jumble all their things together in the pack with few pockets will want to group items together according to how they're used. You can pack different groups of items in large plastic containers with smaller plastic containers within these. For example, put all your morning meal items in one plastic bag and separate the coffee from the cream from the oatmeal from the sugar with smaller plastic baggies. Be sure to carry lots of extra plastic bags since they seem to disappear easily, and double bag items if the baggies are flimsy or if the item they contain could spill and ruin other items and your pack. Extra bags are also convenient for carrying out waste from meals, used toilet paper waste, and dirty clothes.

For larger items, you can use stuff bags sold at sporting goods stores and sturdy plastic bags from shoe shops and dress shops. Stuff bags are heavier, more durable, and more expensive. All perishables should be kept in waterproof containers. It's a good idea to extend this to clothing also. It's easy for things to get wet in rainy country or during a stream crossing. One item that should be carefully protected in a waterproof container are your matches.

One problem the novice backpacker discovers when preparing for her first trip is that most backpacks do not have straps with which to attach the sleeping bag. If you are using a frame pack, bunji cords, elastic cords with hooks on both ends, make ideal connectors. Two cords are usually necessary. Your shovel and foam pad can easily be slipped under the cords. Bunji cords can be purchased in bicycle shops, motorcycle shops, or large sporting goods stores. Buckle straps may also be used and can be purchased in mountaineering and an occasional sporting goods store. Rope can be used but necessitates constant tying and untying. Internal frame packs and some rigid frame packs provide leather casings through which to loop straps and thereby attach a sleeping bag or ice ax. The hood of your pack may also be loose enough to allow you to stow a sleeping bag under it before lashing the top down. Remember that the sleeping bag is one of the heaviest items, however, and try this type of weight distribution before you buy this type of pack. Outside of a few expensive "expedition" or large-sized packs, most do not have enough room in the central compartment to accommodate a sleeping bag plus other gear. Consequently, you will usually have to strap it on the outside. Buy a waterproof stuff sack or use a heavy duty trash bag to protect your sleeping bag from the elements.

If you have a dog, buy or make a dog pack so she can carry her own food. If you have a large, healthy dog, it can carry up to one-half its weight in gear. The weight of the pack may also discourage a dog from chasing wildlife. Sometimes dog packs can get caught in the brush. Dogs can get sores from ill-fitting packs and straps just like people. Check your pet periodically to be sure he or she is not suffering.

Sleeping Bags

Although boots and backpacks are top priorities, sleeping bags are close behind. They are important to ensure that you have a good, comfortable night's sleep and a friendly disposition the next day. There is nothing worse than to have a backpacking companion who isn't getting enough sleep due to a lousy sleeping bag.

Nowadays it is easy to find well made, lightweight, waterproof or water resistant sleeping bags. The weight and type of material depends on where you will be using the bag (cold or hot climates) and your personal needs (how cold you get at night). If you get cold feet at night, you may wish to purchase the mummy bag which tapers towards your feet. Some campers get claustrophobic in this sort of bag. As a compromise, purchase modified mummies that are not as constricting (and not as warm).

You may wish to purchase sleeping bags that zip together. Decide if you want to go this route before you buy a bag, as no bags are universal or adjustable.

Sleeping bags come in several sizes including extra long. If you are over 6 feet tall or if you have a dog that would like a warm spot at night, the extra money for an extra long bag is worth it.

Be sure to buy a stuff bag when you purchase your sleeping bag if one doesn't come with it. The sleeping bag should never get wet (other than by dew). If your bag does become damp, be sure to take the time to dry it. A dry bag may save your life some day.

Sleeping bags come in a variety of fills, the most popular being down or a down mixture. As in down jackets, beware that the quantity of feathers mixed with down is low enough that you are still getting the benefit of the down's warmth. Hollofil II, PolarGuard and some other polyester fill bags are cheaper than down. They are easier to care for and retain their loft better when wet and dirty. However, they do not provide as much insulation per pound as down. For example, a fiberfill bag designed for minus 20 degrees Fahrenheit can weigh up to two pounds more than the equivalent down bag. Fiberfill does not pack as tightly, so it takes more space. Synthetics also do not breathe as well as down. Trapped body heat may keep you warm, but the trade-off is getting sweaty and damp inside the bag—that is unless you loosen the drawstring or zippers to let air circulate.

When you buy a bag it's going to cost some money. Expedition bags can cost about $200 plus. Others, depending on where you purchase them, run between $60 to $150. Check for durability, well-made two-way zippers, and comfortable size. The tight mummy bag is hard to change clothes in although it's a more effective insulator. Check the construction. Layers should never be sewn through and down and fiberfill each have their own most effective, internal construction to insure that the fill will be used to its optimum. The bag should indicate what temperatures it tolerates. If not, you're buying something for the camper or a night at grandma's. If you'll be in cold weather, buy a bag that will tolerate minus 10 degrees Fahrenheit. The warmest expedition bags used on Mt. Everest have minus 40 degree ratings. Three season bags (spring, summer, and fall) should rate between 0 and 10 degrees. Mild weather bags can be between 15 and 40. Remember that a bag can be too hot as well as too cold.

Tents

A tent is not as great a necessity as boots, backpacks, or sleeping bags, but a good one can make your trip infinitely more comfortable, especially in rainy, snowy, windy, or insect-infested country. In some areas such as the wet coastal areas and Alaskan tundra, tents are a necessity because of the insects. In winter camping a tent is extremely important too. On milder journeys, a strong, sturdy tarp, erected with a little ingenuity and consideration for wind direction, can be a cheap and pleasant substitute.

Tents come in all varieties—including size, shape, color, and cost. The most common sizes accommodate two people. There are several one-person tents that are simply a hammock with a roof. The tube tent is extremely cheap but you get exactly what you pay for—next to nothing. These types of tents are not recommended because they do not offer much protection. The best tent size will accommodate you, your gear, and your sleeping bag.

Some tents have a double roof layer. However, the best have a separate cover which does not touch the first roof. This rainfly stretches over the tent and drains away water and provides an air space of insulation.

Ten years ago it was difficult to find a sturdy, lightweight tent. Today they abound; however, they are expensive—

generally between $125 to $250. Cheaper tents just don't do the job—they leak, are heavy, fall over, and fall apart easily. The good ones have lightweight, durable poles. Some have an inner skeleton which means no lines to trip over. Others have outer skeletons. All should have outside loops to peg the tent to the ground.

The size and type of opening of the tent is an important consideration. Netted openings are fairly standard now and keep out the insects. Small, igloo openings are best in the cold and snow. As with sleeping bags, good tents will be labeled to indicate the type of weather they are designed for.

Nylon has pretty much replaced cotton for tent material because of its lighter weight. All tents without rainflys (and sometimes those with rainflys if it's very damp) will wick. If your clothing, sleeping bag, or other gear touches the walls of the tent when the outside of the tent is wet, the contact will draw the water through the tent fiber. All tent seams should be sealed with waterproofing glue which can be purchased in mountaineering outlets.

A rainfly allows the tent material to breathe, letting vapor out. This is better than a single layer waterproofed tent because these do not breathe and moisture from your body can condense inside.

Other features to look for in tents are waterproofed floors that extend up the side of the tent to keep the ground moisture from creeping up into the walls, ventilation flaps, a vestibule or overhanging fly under which you can store dirty boots and other gear, and other inside conveniences such as places to hang lanterns or store small items.

Foam Pads and Mattresses

Foam pads and mattresses have become a must for modern day backpackers. About 20 years ago they were considered a non-essential item due to weight and bulkiness. Today they have been streamlined into lightweight, easy-to-pack, inexpensive necessities.

Besides providing comfort, a foam pad or mattress will keep you warmer. They keep your sleeping bag off the ground serving as a buffer between you and the dew. Because your weight squashes the bag's insulation under you thereby reducing the bag's effectiveness, the mattress or foam pad will help protect you.

Although mattresses usually provide more comfort by providing more distance between your body and the ground, they weigh a lot more and the cost is proportionate. There is a new self-inflating mattress on the market that is lighter than most air mattresses, which saves breath and provides maximum comfort. However it is slightly heavier than foam pads and costs considerably more. Because air circulates freely within an air mattresses' tubes, they offer less warmth than a pad. Foam pads are fairly inexpensive, easy to fold up, and lightweight. The foam pads are more popular than mattresses and can be bought in any store that sells backpack equipment.

One special item to look for in selecting a foam pad or mattress is length. Although a longer length is proportionately heavier and more costly, it also provides added comfort and protection from the dew if you do not use a tent.

Shovels

A shovel may seem like something you could do without but once you've traveled with one, you'll wonder how you ever managed.

A shovel is used 1. to bury human excrement; and 2. to build, remove, and extinguish fires. It is often carried outside the backpack attached to the sleeping bag for easy accessibility. Small, lightweight shovels can be purchased at most backpack stores. Since they are required equipment in some backcountry areas, purchase a shovel with a handle of 12 inches or more. If the shovel is collapsible, check the straightening attachment to be sure it catches and locks properly.

Some persons carry a garden tool or a trowel instead of a shovel for scratching away the ground layer and covering human excrement.

Trenching around a tent or digging deep, long-lasting latrines are no longer acceptable uses for the shovel. Trenching leaves permanent scars on the campsite and human excrement buried below 8 inches will take years to decompose.

Sticks, Broom Handles, and Ice Axes

Some backpackers prefer to hike with long sticks in their hands. When crossing swift or clouded streams of unknown depths and character, a stick helps them keep their balance and feel their way across the stream. When crossing on high logs or narrow shelves, the stick can again serve as a balancer and probe. In snake country it can be used to search the path ahead when there is brush or an unknown object lying in the path. The stick can also be used to wedge aside heavy brush along a trail. Around the campsite the hiking stick can also serve as a backpack prop, beam for a temporary tarp shelter, or prop for a kitchen set-up. A hiking strick is a useful tool for climbing over a rock avalanche that has obliterated the path.

Sticks must be sturdy and long enough to reach your armpit. If they are too large they become unwieldy, and if they are too small they are uncomfortable. They should be sturdy enough to withstand your body weight yet light enough that they aren't an extra weight to carry. They also should have a smooth outer surface so you do not get any splinters.

Two of the best sticks can be made from broom handles or yucca stalks. Once a hiker has found a stick made to her liking, she will reuse it constantly and it will become a permanent part of her backpack equipment.

To be able to safely hike through snow you may wish to purchase an ice ax. If you do purchase one, have someone show you how to use one properly.

The ice ax has three purposes. The first is to serve as an aid, like the stick, for balance, especially when climbing a steep, snowy, or icy hill. The second is to act as a probe to let you determine snow depth. The third function is to save you from a dangerous fall should you lose your footing and slide down the mountain.

The pointed end is used for balance and probing. The ax end is used to do a self-arrest to stop a fall. The idea is to dig the ax into the snow with all your body weight on top. Remember that you have a heavy pack on your back that increases the chances of losing your balance and taking a fall. If you know your trip will take you through a lot of snow country, buy an ice ax and get an expert to take you out for some practice doing self-arrests.

An ice ax can also be one of your more fun purchases. It can be used to perform a sport called glissading. Using your feet as a pair of skis and the ice ax as a rudder and for balance behind the hips, bend at the knees and head down a steep icy or snowy incline. You will slide down the mountain at great speeds. This is great fun however, do not do this with your pack on your back. As a word of caution, be sure your stopping spot is not a rock boulder. Once you get going it is hard to stop.

Stoves

Stoves are a necessary part of your equipment although you do not need to buy one immediately. During your first few backpack trips with other experienced hikers, share their camp stove. Offer to carry the extra gas since they are carrying the stove.

There are a variety of stoves on the market so, again look for durability, lightweight, lighting ease, fuel capability, and cost features. The most popular stoves on the market today are Scandinavian brands that have pots especially designed to fit the stove in order to achieve optimum heat efficiency.

Do not leave the store with a new stove until you have learned to use it safely. A stove can explode into flames burning your face, hair and clothing.

When buying a stove, purchase a lightweight container to carry extra fuel. Be sure the container has a tight lid so it will not leak.

A stove should be used where open fires are prohibited, above timberlines, whenever camping near alpine lakes or near fragile ecosystems, during emergencies, in areas of wood scarcity, and wherever they are required by law. Always provide fire protection when using your stove by clearing away vegetation around it, keeping it balanced on flat surfaces, and having bare soil or rock beneath.

Cooking Utensils

Fire-blackened pots are just one of the inconveniences of cooking over an open fire. For good pots, a layer of thick soap dried on the outside of the pot will make the soot easier to remove. You don't have to scrub the outside of the pot each time you use it, otherwise you might be cleaning pots the whole trip instead of enjoying the outdoors. Keep pots in a plastic bag so the soot won't ruin your other gear.

If you don't want to worry about cleaning pots, take coffee cans. Secure a wire handle to the top so you can pull them out of the fire easily. Or in lieu of a wire handle (and easier) use removable broad pliers which can be purchased separately in backpacking supply stores. For medium-sized coffee cans, a Sierra cup fits perfectly as a lid. When you return home, throw the cans away.

Take a long wooden spoon or a stick stripped of its bark to stir the food with so you do not get too close to the fire. A small, lightweight backpacker's grill which can be used for placing pots over the fire or for directly broiling fish and other items is nice to have along.

Food

While the mind can wax poetic over the possibilities of trail delicacies, what you should take depends on how much you can carry. In addition to packing enough for three meals a day, take enough snacks for a mid-morning and mid-afternoon respite. Backpacking uphill is estimated to burn between 500 to 600 calories per hour. Contrast this with sleeping (34 calories), and gardening (96 calories).

If you're making a difficult trip, you may want the specialized dehydrated, freeze-dried backpackers meals. Although these are outrageously expensive considering they're mostly carbohydrates, they do weigh less and take less space. Do some creative substituting by visiting the convenience section of the supermarket. Although you have to repackage them, you can use dried soups, spaghetti dinners, macaroni and cheese.

The kind of food to pack for strenuous outdoor activity is the sort you probably avoid at home. Protein, for example, is important for rebuilding the body's cells but is normally not used as a fuel during exercise of any kind. Unless you're on a long trip and are extremely lean, you don't especially need much of it. Carbohydrates, which include all sugars and starches (noodles, crackers, cereal, fruit) are essential. If you're planning a short strenuous trip, such as a one-day climbing venture, stock up on your carbs. The reason for including a lot of these goodies in your day pack is because as the intensity of the exercise increases and duration decreases, the body uses more carbohydrates. A word of caution about sugars: too much sugar taken in a short period of time retards the rate at which the sugar in the stomach is absorbed into the blood stream, and actually delays its availability for energy use. Small frequent snacks and liquids with about a teaspoon of sugar per quart (2.5 grams per liter) are the best to sustain energy. Sugars that are easy for the body to break down are even better. These include dried fruits and honey.

If you are planning a trip of more than a day include some fats. Avocados, nuts, butter, cheese, and peanut butter are good sources as are any other foods which are oily, fatty, or greasy. Fat helps sustain energy and is essential for endurance exercise. Some mountaineers take along cooking oil for this reason. Although it sounds disgusting, they down a couple of ounces to keep their strength up. Although your body uses carbohydrates the most at first, it slowly yields to consuming fat as the exercise continues. Fat which is immediately available in the bloodstream—meaning that which you eat—will reward you with a superior performance. However, since the use of fat generally starts about three to four hours after you've eaten it, the rewards won't be immediate.

Carbohydrates are still important after five days in the field because they ward off muscle exhaustion. This is so even if there is plenty of fat left to the body as fuel. A low carbohydrate diet leads to muscle exhaustion. So, even if you're overweight or overfat, take along the carbohydrates.

Among favorite trail foods women in our survey named were nuts, seeds, dried fruit, peanut butter, instant soups mixed with grains, packets of instant oats or rice mixed with milk for breakfast, raw fruit, cheese, dried salami, oysters and other canned meats, granola, fresh fruit, and fresh vegetables.

Mary Lou Reed, former chairwoman of the Idaho Conservation League, said meals can be vastly improved by some light additions such as croutons and Parmesan cheese for onion soup, bay leaves and basil for stew, and freeze-dried meat and vegetable flakes for grocery store casserole mixes and stews and soups.

Mary Ann Green, a fire lookout during the summer and excellent cook both on the trail and off, regularly bakes upside-down cakes by layering the bottom of the cook kit with dried fruit and some water, then pouring in instant cake batter, covering the container and surrounding it with the embers of the campfire.

One woman takes along alfalfa seeds and sprouts them in her pack. Another suggests her specialty of stuffed squash. Using a rice mixture as a stuffing, she cooks the squash in the same manner Mary Ann bakes her cakes.

Vicki Montgomery, a United States Forest Service employee, has a master mix she regularly carries on the trail. With this she makes pancakes, biscuits, and pies from foraged berries. She says if you run out of bread, you can make a really good cheese pancake using wholewheat flour, powdered milk, a little salt, brewer's yeast, wheat germ, bran and maybe some soy flour, powdered eggs, and some baking soda mixed in proportions to a regular biscuit or pancake recipe. Add oil and water to the right consistency to cook.

Although this verges on sacrilege among some backpacking circles, many people regularly carry some canned foods such as stews, meatballs, and canned spaghett. They eat the heavy items early in the trip. Like many, they save the small tins of turkey, shrimp, or chicken to supplement what they consider to be the generally thin gruel offered by backpackers' freeze-dried fare or the noodles and broth sold in the grocery stores.

Water

Without a doubt, the favorite trail drink is cool spring water. Close seconds are teas and instant drinks. Kool-Aid also serves to palpatize some bad tasting sulphur waters. Other drinks mentioned were hot chocolate, hot Jello, and bouillon cubes which are comforting in cold weather. Many equate liquor with a warm night in camp, while others disapprove of it strongly.

A final and important note on nutrition, be aware of your salt and liquid intake. Most dehydrated foods contain a lot of salt. Processed foods also contain quite a bit. Perhaps the notion of downing salt tablets to prevent dehydration evolved from the trapper and early mountainman era when processed foods were not available and salt was at a premium. Not so today, leave the salt tablets on the counter. Under mild wilderness conditions, it's possible to get too much salt. You'll know you're getting too much if your ankles and wrists start to swell. Dark urine may also indicate too much salt. A vegetarian or someone who avoids processed foods in some ways mimics the low-salt diet of the pioneers and may need a supplement.

Salt, along with potassium and magnesium, is important for backcountry activity. These electrolytes conduct messages from the nerves to the muscles and are important for coordination. If you'll be going for many days without fresh fruits and juices, take along an electrolyte replacement (ERG) to mix with water. These are found in mountaineering, health food, and sporting goods stores. Although the amount of water a woman needs in a hot environment has not been studied, some conclusions can be drawn from the experiences of men. Since women do not sweat as much as men, they may not need as much water or salt.

Under extreme circumstances such as strenuous activity at temperatures above one-hundred degrees, men can lose up to two quarts of water in a single hour. This kind of water loss, and milder forms, can lead to heat exhaustion. Heat exhaustion is not uncommon even while on an average backpacking or river trip.

Water bottles should be leak proof, easy to fill, fit in an outside pocket or other readily available spot where they will remain cool, and be lightweight. If you are hiking where water is scarce and your bottle leaks, you may be faced with a life and death situation. One way to be sure your bottle doesn't leak is to fill it with water and turn it upside down.

Water is so easily available to us most of the time, that we tend to overlook its importance. Although it is generally available for backcountry use in the eastern parts of the United States, in the west range wars have been fought over it and an entirely different set of laws has evolved regarding its use.

Water weighs a lot: two pounds per quart. Four quarts is about what you need per day. That means eight pounds if you have to carry it, generally more than a tent, and about twice as much as your sleeping bag. Plan ahead on where water will, not should, be. Get to know the difference between intermittent and continual streams. Are you hiking in a lava formation? Since lava is porous, that lake on the map might not be there when you stumble up to it with a dry tongue. The best solution is to ask around ahead of time. Some areas don't present much of a problem since the trail winds beside a river. However, often the trail is at the top of the river canyon rather than the bottom. To be safe, carry some water along even if hiking near a river.

Is backcountry water contaminated? A safe assumption is yes. The more so, the more it's used. Even remote areas offer the risk of disease from any number of organisms. Chemical contamination should be suspected in areas of mining, industrial, and agricultural activity.

Chemical contaminants make their presence known through smell and taste. The presence of frogs, tadpoles, and insect life is a good indication the water is not heavy with chemicals. This is a good rule of thumb in nonindustrialized areas, since chemical contaminants can occur naturally too.

Biological contaminants include bacteria, protozoa, and viruses. Virulent forms of bacteria result from human waste.

Although the common E. coli bacteria is usually the culprit if the water makes you sick, the serious backpacker's disease of giardiasis is becoming increasingly common. This disease is caused by the protozoa giardia lamblia, a simple one-celled animal. It can be carried by most warm-blooded animals. Is there a beaver pond on your stream? Is there fresh snowmelt that could have washed miniscule particles of animal feces into the water? Do horses use the trail? Is livestock grazed in the area? If so, boil the water for twenty minutes. Longer if you're above 10,000 feet since water boils at lower temperatures at altitude and it takes longer to kill the organism.

Check with city, county land management agency, or state

health officials to see what the incidence of giardiasis has been. In most industrialized countries, doctors are supposed to report these cases. Without casting aspersions on the medical profession, some doctors probably don't report isolated cases or misdiagnose them because the symptoms are so similar to other maladies. If you do get sick while or after visiting the backcountry and suspect contaminated water, tell the doctor. That way she'll know to run the right tests.

Giardiasis symptoms are similar to a host of other diseases coming from contaminated water including diarrhea, flatulence, nausea, belching, stomach cramps, and vomiting. They can lead to dehydration, and in general, make you miserable. Since the giardia go through a cyst stage, the symptoms take a week or more to show up. They are also resistant to the common forms of chemical treatment including iodination or chlorination. This is why health officials are concerned about them.

Most of the bacterial organisms show symptoms in six to forty-eight hours. If you get sick right away, one of these, not giardiasis, is probably responsible.

Viruses such as hepatitis in the water also result from human waste. As anyone who has had the flu knows, these viruses do not respond well to treatment with antibiotics. Boiling or chemical treatment will kill them.

Bacterial diseases can be treated with antibiotics, while giardiasis can be treated with atabrine and metranidizol (flagyl). While a doctor will probably be willing to prescribe an antibiotic for your first aid kit, you'll meet with reluctance on the last two. Flagyl has been implicated as carcinogenic (cancer causing), and atabrine can turn your skin yellow—like too many carrots.

Boiling your water is the safest insurance, but admittedly, it's a hassle. If you've checked the area out, and have no reason to suspect giardiasis, you can probably get by with chemical purification of the water.

Although halazone (chlorine) tablets are still widely used, iodine treatment is the most effective. All it requires is two drops of tincture of iodine per cup, or three to four drops per quart, and up to six drops per quart for heavy contamination.

This should be followed by a wait of about twenty minutes to allow the chemical to take action.

Filtration straws can be purchased from mountaineering outlets and if used properly, will clear the water of bacterial organisims. A more elaborate system is needed for expeditions.

If you're planning a trek where the pureness of the public water supply is uncertain, check for chloera, dysentery, typhoid fever, hepatitis, and amebiasis. If you employ porters, they should be checked also. Checking means a culture done of the stool. Since this is unlikely, you will need a good translator and honest porters. Keep your eye on anyone who handles your group's food or water.

Joyce Lee English, a woman who has camped in Mexico, says to drink only purified water (and icecubes) and to wash fruit and vegetables in a weak solution of bleach or iodine and water. She says they also ate very little locally prepared food. Dairy products obtained locally are suspect or any food containing them such as bread and cheeses. Meats and probably all other food should be regarded with suspicion unless you make sure they are fresh and are cooked long enough. Joyce got sick on her first trip and cites Pepto Bismol as a must.

Clothing

"Dear WW:
Is anyone out there getting as tired as I am of not being able to find work boots or gloves small enough to fit me? Of hardhats that fall over my eyes when the band is as tight as it will go? Of women's cowboy boots too narrow for anyone with a full complement of toes and available only in fluorescent hand-tooled alligator or turquoise-and-silver baroque when a nice, simple tan roughout style would do?

How about workshirts and wool shirts and down parkas that are too tight around the hips, while there's room for a party in the shoulders? Or am I just a crank, a discontented misfit because I wince and grit my teeth whenever I am forced, through lack of choice, to buy a flimsy "ladies'" version of an outdoor garment which isn't nearly as warm or durable or functional (no pockets) as the standard men's item? Those "ladies'" items begin to disintegrate on the third or fourth use and, to add insult to injury, generally cost even more than the comparable men's item (that cute little floral pattern isn't free).

Well, after years of freezing my butt off while my male companions are comfortable because their long underwear is twice as thick as mine (cute floral patterns have never been known for their ability to retain BTUs), I am mad enough to do something about it. Never again will I wear out my (ill-fitting—had to get a man's size) boots, searching endlessly for a store that carries a decent pair of work gloves in small sizes.

Perhaps you women in the Bay Area and other such metropolises cannot relate to my aggravation. I am aware that some of the more elite mountaineering supply companies, who have outlets in large cities, manufacture women's clothing very similar to men's. But this clothing is expensive and often impossible to obtain in rural areas. What we need is for average, everyday clothing and sporting goods stores everywhere to carry the same items they now carry in men's sizes in women's sizes as well—with the same basic durability and functionality, but tailored to fit women.

Our basic problem is that manufacturers and retailers, for the most part, aren't aware of our existence. These guys aren't "keep her barefoot and pregnant in the kitchen" misogynists, they're businessmen. If a messenger from God appeared before them and informed them there are hordes of lady loggers and female mountaineers clamoring to buy their products, the market would be flooded with petite-size cork boots and women's wool pants and shirts. They need to know that there are a lot more of us out here than they presently suspect; that we don't just accompany hubby on weekend fishing trips in the family RV but we hike, climb, canoe, work, hunt, farm, and ranch in the outdoors, and we need clothing that meets the demands of our work and play. (1)

Patricia Corry
Montana
Women in the Wilderness Quarterly

This letter to the editor of a women's wilderness journal describes the common plight of the serious outdoorswoman who needs serious outdoors gear. This problem is aggravated if a woman needs to pack a wider range of clothing due to greater sensitivity to heat and cold.

Even in very hot country during the day, there is usually a drastic decrease in temperature once the sun sets. Usually prepare for 30 degree weather, even when the trip begins in 100 degree temperatures. You never know when the weather will change. Even if temperatures during a sudden rainstorm only drop to 50 degrees, if there's a strong wind the chill factor will bring it down to 20 degrees or colder.

When one woman was hiking with her family on a day trip in hot, semi-desert country in California, clouds brought an unexpected hail storm. Temperatures dropped drastically from 80 degrees to 20° Fahrenheit or lower and a strong wind whipped against them. Without their jackets, their wet skin, fanned by the wind, made them begin to shiver violently. Although they stepped up their pace, they could not regain the lost body heat. Luckily, a shelter found at the crucial moment saved them from hypothermia.

Another woman had a similar experience during the "mild" month of June in Idaho's Snake River Mountains. After benign temperatures of 70 degrees Fahrenheit the first day, it proceeded to snow for a day and a half. However, all was well as she had taken the correct clothing.

The best way to plan your clothing is to adhere to the "layered" principal which translates into "put it on," "take it off," "put it on again." A typical layer is a T-shirt, a long-sleeved cotton shirt, a wool shirt, a down vest or wool sweater, and a down parka. Add to this a poncho, a pair of long pants and a pair of shorts, some underwear and socks, and you are ready to take a simple summer trip. Some people prefer no change of T-shirts or other items on trips since they take too much room. Others take an extra T-shirt and underwear for aesthetics (smell).

Weight and bulk are other major considerations in choosing clothing. Remember, however, not to overpack. You are not headed for a resort. Instead choose clothes for comfort and survival. Always plan on the layered principal of lightweight inner clothing building to heavier outer clothing. Weight and bulk are other major considerations in buying backpack clothes. If you are going on a long hike, you will need all available space in the pack for food. As always, keep the weight at a minimum while still carrying all the essentials.

The two favorite fabrics for backpack clothing are wool and cotton. Some combinations of these with other materials such as dacron are also successful. Wool is excellent in cold or rainy weather. It absorbs heat, sheds water, and dries quickly. Unfortunately, some people are allergic to wool or find it itches. Cotton absorbs and disperses moisture. It helps provide a 98.6 degree atmosphere next to the skin thereby aiding the cooling process in hot weather and the warming process in cold weather. Generations of backpackers swear by these fabrics to the point that polyester is a sacrilege and backcountry faux pas.

In cold, rainy weather when you need added warmth, wool is the best material because it allows you to stay warm yet it releases the sweat through its loose weave. Wool is also water-resistant and sheds wetness for a long period of time before becoming soaked.

Jackets

Major things to look for in an outer jacket are warmth capabilities, pockets, hood, and weight. Although down is highly praised as a fill, it dries slowly once soaked. Down has the advantage of being lightweight as well as being super warm. Holofill is much cheaper than down, is also lightweight and warm, can be washed, sheds water, and will dry properly afterwards. Some new fibers are beginning to find a following. Most, however, don't breathe as well as down. Here again, price is a factor. The synthetics in this case are cheaper than all those bits of fluff plucked off an entrapped goose. If you decide to invest in down, make sure that the outer fabric is strong enough to withstand wear and tear, is Ripstop (won't run like a pair of nylons), and that the quantity of feathers mixed with the down is low enough that you won't be in a constant state of molt. Feathers and down are most definitely not the same. What's passed off as down is often feathers. These are fine for keeping birds dry and airborn, but it's the underlayer of down that keeps them warm.

Other items to look for in protective outer jackets are sleeves that tighten (Velcro or buttons) so that the air, snow, insects, brush, rain, and cold won't creep up your arms and down your hands; zippers or buttons that are sturdy and won't come apart easily; neck covering (zippers or buttons up high); and below-the-waist-protection, again so that the air, snow, insects, brush, rain, or cold won't creep up your waist.

Waterproof materials are best where precipitation is common. Water repellent materials are adequate where precipitation is periodic.

It would, at first thought, seem advisable to take rain gear such as is worn by equestrians or sailors. These are heavy slickers, often designed as pants and jacket. However, such raingear is generally vetoed because it is too hot. As you hike in rain or snow, the body releases heat from the energy expended and in airtight rain gear this heat builds up and causes intense discomfort. Such gear is also cumbersome and heavy.

The lightweight, yet durable, backpacker's poncho is the best rain gear to take although heat and perspiration will also build up in it. An advantage to the backpacker's poncho is that it is made to cover the backpack. During a rainstorm, the added protection of the poncho will help ensure that the articles within the backpack remain dry.

New fibers such as Gore-Tex are looked upon with suspicion in some quarters. Gore-Tex is a water-repellent petro-based fabric which, through an ingenious weave, keeps outside water out yet allows sweat from the inside to evaporate. This may sound like defiance of the second law of thermodynamics. Someone all decked out in Gore-Tex jackets and pants is making an economic statement whether she intends to or not—Gore-Tex is expensive. In some quarters, principally among persons who keep up with the latest equipment trends, Gore-Tex is an asset. Implications aside, if you can afford it, Gore-Tex is excellent for rainy areas and winter activities where a parka is too much and a windbreaker too little.

Gor-Tex is also not regarded by many to hold up well under moist conditions of long duration. Many people say it leaks. Another synthetic material, Thinsulite, is good for short trips in which the body needs to be less encumbered as in climbing. However, it is not as warm as down.

Pants

With your legs covered you have protection from sunburn and sunheat; protection from mosquitoes, flies, ticks, chiggers, and other pests; a shield from scratches, lacerations, stinging nettles, poison oak or sumac; warmth in cold weather; and coolness, under certain conditions, in hot weather.

However, many backpackers also wear short pants when the right conditions exist. Advocates of short pants do not like the feeling of encumbrances about their legs caused by long pants. They also like the healthy look of a suntan. Short pants seem cooler by allowing rapid evaporation of perspiration.

Short pants are best worn when there is no vegetation and no bugs; when you're on a good trail that is easy to follow with little danger of falling or tripping; and when there is good weather, a rare combination indeed.

Contrary to expectations, people absorb heat more directly when exposed to the sun with bare skin than when protected with light, reflective clothing. Wearing shorts can actually cause the body to sweat more than wearing long, loose pants. The Arabs wear long, flowing robes in the hot desert for this reason. Still, many backpackers take a pair of short pants along and don them at every opportunity.

In summer seasons in "warm" country wear short pants when it's wet although not in a biting cold wind. If it's raining, long pants will get wet, grubby, heavy, and stick to your skin. Long pants will encourage heat loss from your body because the cold moisture will draw the heat away from your skin. Even if you wear a long poncho, it will not protect the feet and legs from brushing against the grasping wet vegetation along the trail or from the moisture blown by the wind that often accompanies rain.

Rather than play on-again, off-again pants roulette wear short pants when you are making numerous stream crossings. They're also fun for fishing trips when you want to wade into streams.

If you hike in the rain, or when you cross cold streams, remember that cool water drains the body heat very rapidly. When you stop for a break, immediately dry your legs and cover them to retain body heat until you resume walking. To dry off, use a cotton bandanna. When hiking, carry the bandanna in your belt loop and it will dry very quickly.

Slim Woodruff wears a pair of long pants with zippers around each leg so the leg can be removed leaving shorts. This way she not only saves weight, but she doesn't have to vanish into the bushes to change. If trying this, she advises, use baggy pants which will fit over your boots and zippers sewn so as not to touch the skin.

In cold weather or where weather quickly changes in temperament, take a valuable extra pair of long pants in case one gets wet. Baggy, practical, warm wool pants can often be purchased cheaply at army surplus stores.

Pants should be loose. Tight pants, encouraged by modern fashions and even some backpack equipment catalogs, can constrict blood movement to and from your legs. They are also uncomfortable and limit freedom of movement. Women pictured in tight Levis have difficulty bounding over a boulder field. They're also probably having heat problems since the tight sheath of denim traps body heat next to the skin. If tight pants get wet, it will take them longer to dry especially if they're made of denim.

Several teenage girls on an expedition in an ice cave got their tight jeans wet and were the first to develop hypothermia. Their damp pants against their bodies quickly lowered their body temperatures to a dangerous level.

Although many women are staunch supporters of denim for wilderness-wear because it is so durable, the trade-off is the extra weight and extra drying time.

Pants with a lot of accessible, deep pockets are handy. Many essentials an be carried this way when exploring. Recommended pocket stuffers (although you'll quickly find your own) are matches, tissue paper (serviceable as toilet paper or fire starter), bandanna, pocket knife, map, backcountry permit, and snacks. A Sierra cup can be tied to your bandanna at the belt loop. Around the waist you can tie a lightweight, rainproof parka or poncho. All of this won't weigh much and could mean the difference in a survival situation should you get separated from your pack.

Gaiters are also a good item to take in snowy or rainy country although they are extra weight to consider. Gaiters keep the snow and water out of your boots and off your lower legs, protecting your pants and socks from the dampness. They are waterproofed, zippered accessories that attach to the boot and around the knee. They also help keep your boots and pants clean.

Sometimes backpacking in mixed company can be awkward. In highly used areas it's not much fun to get caught in the line-of-sight of a troop of intrepid Boy Scouts with your pants around your knees. No simple zipping of the fly will get you out of this one and it's nigh impossible to recover your pants and your dignity before the merry Scouts are upon you. Or maybe you're cross-country skiing and herringboned off the trail for a rest stop. What to your wondering eyes does appear but the vice president of academic affairs of the university where you're employed. He's amused; after all, it's not his fanny glowing for public view in the crisp winter air.

To solve this perennial problem, some clothing manufacturers are making hiking pants with Velcro crotches for women. The inseam is flanked with Velcro for easy access without having to get undressed. You can make your own adaptation if you know how to sew. Added to this is the possibility of inserting snaps in the crotch of your underwear.

In addition to providing privacy, the Velcro crotch also reduces exposure of your skin unnecessarily in subzero temperatures. In situations where frostbite is a real possibility for any exposed skin, some women have been known to use catheters. The tube can then be run out the fly of the pants when necessary, mimicking the manner in which a man urinates.

Gloves

Women, at least small or average-sized women, do run the risk of getting cold hands and feet faster than men in prolonged exposure. This is because a small person does not have as great a thermal mass as a large person. Much like a small object cools faster than a large object, a small person will become cold faster than a large one. This is especially true of your extremities, since in very cold weather your body will be busy keeping your vital organs warm and will sacrifice your hands and feet in the process.

Whenever there is the slightest chance of cool weather or cold nights, take a pair of gloves. They can serve as hand-warmers, potholders, and can add protection from splinters when wood gathering, or from sharp thorns and poison ivy with overgrown vegetation along trails or cross crountry. When using tools, work gloves will help prevent blisters and other injuries.

For women with small hands, work gloves designed for small hands can be ordered from a hardware or drygoods store. Children's sizes will occasionally fit. Most stores don't keep them in their regular stock. They can be mail ordered from American Working Women's Supply Company, Box 100–M, Deer Park, New York 11729.

Nylon undergloves are helpful for keeping your hands warm under an outer pair of heavier gloves or mittens.

Head Protection

During your first few nights in cold weather, you may find yourself curled up inside your bag suffocating. This is the common "get-my-head-out-of-the-cold" syndrome that beginning backpackers experience. It is a rude awakening to discover the dew settling all over you in the early morning. Even if you have a tent, the cold will be felt as the dew settles outside. This, coupled with the cold night air, will numb your nose and breathe down your neck sending you into paroxysms of shivers. It also makes it hard to sleep. There are two solutions to this problem. One is to bury your head inside the bag in a cramped, suffocating position. The other is to wear a warm hat.

Proportionately, most body heat is lost from the head. This is because the blood supply to the head is great and is constantly at full capacity. While the blood traveling to other parts of the body diminishes when you're sleeping, the supply to your head never rests because if it did, you'd go into a coma. If you wear a hat, your whole body will feel warmer because it is not wasting all that excess heat on your uncovered head.

Besides wearing a hat to bed on a cold night, tie a bandanna around your neck. This will not only keep your neck warm but will also block drafts trying to creep under your collar.

A hat will also protect your head from direct hot sun for coolness and skin protection. The skin of people constantly exposed to the sun ages quicker, becomes leathery, and sometimes develops cancer.

A large, wide-brimmed hat (like a cowboy hat) will not work unless you pin the back portion up behind your head. Otherwise your pack will constantly knock it down over your nose or create an annoying rubbing action. A better solution is a tennis hat with a narrow headband and broad bill. This hat is not good, however, if your hair part is exposed to the sun. Hats used by the military in the tropics (Dr. Livingston, I presume) had an inner band that kept the lightweight hat away from the head's surface thereby providing ventilation. Other hat solutions are baseball and crew hats. Loose wooven straw is a good material for hiking in hot weather because moisture can escape through the weave and because it is lightweight. Nylon and synthetic hats retain moisture and heat. Wool hats are best in the cold weather as they allow moisture to escape while retaining the heat.

Summer hats should be white or another light color to reflect away rather than absorb the sun's rays. Winter hats should be dark colors for the opposite reason.

Besides providing protection from the sun and warmth on a cold night, hats have an extra bonus: they keep the bugs away. A straw hat with long pieces of straw fringed around the edge kept one woman from losing her sanity during an epidemic of blackflies along a trail in the Baker Wilderness in Oregon one August. Argentine cowboys wear hats fringed with dangling corks to flick the insects away. Some sporting good stores sell nets that attach to hats and protect the face from insect bombardment.

A final use for a hat is pure aesthetics. It is difficult and usually unecological to wash your hair in the backcountry. A hat hides your matted, unkempt hair.

Underwear

Most women wear nylon or other synthetic underwear. This is

very impractical when hiking. Synthetics absorb and retain heat. Perspiration buildup from a vigorous hike remains trapped in this type of underwear. This can matter a great deal in very cold weather since it adds to the loss of essential body heat and forces your body to work harder to keep warm when you need all your energy to keep moving.

Underwear should be cotton which will absorb the moisture. A loose weave is better than a tight weave, since it will allow moisture to escape and, in cold weather, will help trap a layer of warm air next to the skin.

A bra is important for backpacking use since you need support. Like in running, your breasts will be in constant motion. Numerous manufacturers make a cotton bra. The simpler the bra, the greater your comfort. Broad straps do not roll and twist as easily as thin straps when they are constantly rubbed by the pack straps. Be sure that the buckle or tie of the bra is not rubbed by the pack. Several runner's magazines advertise special bras which provide support, comfort, and a sturdy, but not binding fit.

When suddenly exposed to intense heat, many women's breasts swell and/or feel very painful. Unfortunately, not wearing a bra will provide little relief as this is not the problem. It will take your body a while to adjust. Drinking a lot of water and being sure to have the proper amount of daily salt is helpful in speeding up adjustment.

Old underwear with loose elastic is ideal in chigger or tick country. These insects often burrow along the bra or panty line where the blood is more accessible due to the constriction of the elastic. When checking for ticks, this is a good place to start.

If you should ever get a firefighting job, the men will not remember to warn you about nylon underwear since most men wear cotton. When exposed to flame, nylon burns and sticks to skin like glue. Cotton burns quickly and falls off. Professional firefighters wear either special firefighting clothing (called nomex) or cotton pants, shirts, and underwear. Remember, the cotton is also cooler in heat.

Camping in the snow, during winter, or at high elevations should cause serious consideration for taking a pair of longjohns. Fine-wool longjohns can be found in the lingerie sections of department stores. Dime stores carry ribbed and popcorn cotton long underwear at inexpensive prices. Keep your feet warmer by slipping a pair of inner soles made of felt, foam, or wool into your boots.

Footwear

Boots are one of the most expensive and most important items you will purchase when preparing for the backcountry. If your feet are not comfortable, you are in for a very painful trip.

Rule number one is to *never* rent or borrow someone else's boots. Rule number two is to break in your boots as thoroughly as possible before taking a demanding trip.

A shoe salesman will generally tell you that it doesn't matter if you buy a man's boot. Don't believe it. Many women have narrower ankles than men and a boot made for women allows for this difference. If a woman wears a man's boots, she can expect to get blisters on her ankles. As a general rule, Vibram-soled boots are usually best because they provide traction, "cling" to rocks better, and wear well.

Another favorite shoe pitch is to tell the buyer to put more socks on or take socks off depending on whether the boot feels too big or too little. Most people wear two pairs of socks. The inner or liner pair is generally strong, lightweight cotton to absorb sweat. The outer pair is heavier and made of thick cotton or wool which cushions the rub of the heavy boot against the foot. Three pairs are too bulky and one pair isn't enough protection.

Be sure to buy polish and weatherproofing kits for proper care of your boots. A liquid silicone preparation is recommended by Eastern Mountain Sports, Inc. (EMS), a national equipment retailer. This makes your boots moderately water repellent while allowing them to breathe. A silicone wax, like Sno-Seal, is good in the winter. Greases and saddle soaps tend to soften the leather too much. If the leather gets too dry, the EMS editors suggest spot applications of boot oil.

Carry an extra set of shoelaces with you. There is nothing more agonizing than to break an irreparable shoelace fifty miles in the backcountry. If you carry nylon cord (used in bear country to hang food in a tree), it can serve as a temporary shoelace.

When your boots get wet, try to wear them dry. If not, dry at air temperature. Avoid rapid drying next to the campfire. This promotes cracking and deterioration of the leather, and even worse, it causes the boots to lose their shape.

Some women may be changing from high heels to boots. High heels cause the Achilles tendon to shorten decreasing the range of motion of your ankles and legs. When you switch to boots, the result will be pain. You'll notice this first on downhill stretches. Downhill hiking is especially hard on the feet and the legs. Blisters will often develop because, not only are your feet and lower legs carrying all your weight, but also the impact of each footfall is greater. To avoid these problems break in your boots (and feet) and maybe consider giving up high heels before an extended trip into the wilderness.

Even if your new boots mesh with your feet like parts of a precision camera, if you are a beginner, you're almost certain to get blisters. Band-Aids are absolutely worthless when it comes to blisters. The best protection against blisters is preventive maintenance; patch your trouble spots with moleskin before your feet sprout blisters. Moleskin is an inexpensive adhesive, a felt material, which provides a buffer between your skin, your socks, and the hard boot rubbing against them. It can be purchased in any drug store or mountaineering outlet and should be part of your first aid kit. Apply it to places where your backpack, paddle, or rope may rub against your skin too.

If you wait until after you have blisters to apply the moleskin, it will still effectively prevent further damage. However, it will stick to the wound and it may be quite painful when it's time to remove the moleskin. Many runners and climbers use tincture of benzoin by applying it to their skin ahead of time to toughen the skin and thereby prevent blisters.

Slim Woodruff recommends foot slips instead of moleskin. These prevent blisters and have been used by football teams for years. Woodruff writes:

> They come in large sizes but if they are too large they will fold over without causing discomfort. They are worn on the bare foot

under the sock, and while they feel slippery and odd at first, once they warm up and moisten up with sweat (ecch) they mold to the foot and you forget they are there. As it says in the Handds packet, they can be washed. I usually wear them dirty and use them for a five day hike, then give them the toss. I have only ever used the toe section, since I have some trouble with the ball of my foot. This is why I prefer the foot slips to the Hannds, which are one piece. Also our cost from Adams Plastics is about 15 cents per foot slip, as opposed to wholesale cost of 80 cents for Handds. However you have to be a dealer and buy in bulk to get the foot slips from Adams, and the Handds are sold in a few hiking stores, ours, the Trailhead in Buena Vista, Colorado, for one. They seem to be catching on very slowly. People are afraid to try them. But when I talk someone on a trip into using them, they are very impressed. Give them a try if you are having any trouble with blisters. I have used them to break in new boots, or when I get blisters running. Or, as happens every spring, when my body is in shape but my feet are not yet broken back into wearing hiking boots.

Handds can be purchased from Handds Distribution Company, Inc., 327 East Wayne, #200-B, Fort Wayne, Indiana 46802.

Some backpackers will tell you that you might as well hike barefoot as wear tennis shoes. Though this is an exaggeration, tennis shoes do not give the ankle and arch support needed, nor will they protect feet from rocks and vegetation. Although some backpackers are staunch advocates of tennis shoes, they also run the risk of sprains, shinsplints, cuts, bruises, and other maladies. For the best footwear and care, buy a good boot.

There are sensitive hiking areas that have received so much use by lug-soled boots that deep trenches have developed. In these and other environmentally sensitive areas, concerned hikers are changing to smooth-soled shoes with ankle supports to reduce impact. However, even the light hiking boots carried by mountaineering outlets generally have lug-soles. If you are planning to hike in such an area, such as the Sierras in California, contact a nearby conservation organization and ask what sort of shoe they recommend to minimize impact.

When you arrive at your destination, remove your heavy boots and put on something more comfortable for campground puttering. Some people carry a pair of tennis shoes for this purpose. These can also serve as waders for stream crossings.

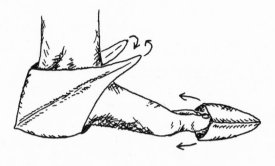

FOOT   SLIPS

"HANDDS"

A barefooted stream crossing is a painful and sometimes dangerous experience. The water is cold and rocks are sharp. If the water is flowing strong, you may have to wear your boots to provide an anchor and balance when fording the stream.

If you know for sure that your trail will have bridges or no stream crossings, then rubber thongs and moccasins are cheap and lightweight. When wearing thongs or moccasins, keep your feet warm with a pair of socks. Some women carry an extra pair of old, thick socks to wear over thermal booties as camp shoes. This keeps the booties clean enough to wear to bed on cold nights.

Socks

It never hurts to be a fanatic when it comes to socks. When your feet are wet and cold, you are wet and cold. Pack at least one extra pair of both liner and outer socks. (These can also serve as mittens if need be.) Always keep one pair dry—don't depend on good weather and wash both sets at once. Otherwise, you might be stuck with wet socks—no big catastrophe in a drive-in campground but a very unhappy one if the temperature dips and you have a long way to hike.

One woman started carrying more than three pairs of socks because of memorable hiking experiences in the Cascades of western Washington. It rains a lot there. When the sun does shine, it's the most beautiful place—babbling, full streams; lush, green vegetation; tall, stately trees; and jagged, tree-capped mountains. But when it rains, there is nothing more dismal. The problem with the rain in western Washington is that it really doesn't rain—it drizzles—constantly. In most places, the clouds gather, darken, and then let go in one big nasty torrent or several nasty torrents called rain. Usually there is a pause before the next downpour begins. But in the Cascades, it drizzles. When it rains constantly, understandably your socks get wet. But they are not just wet from the rain. They are wet from sloshing through swollen streams, spluttering through muddy trails that often become streams, and brushing past water saturated vegetation. Actually your socks aren't just wet—they are soaked.

If you are on a ten-day hike, and it is constantly drizzling, it soon becomes evident that three pairs of socks are not enough. The two pair you wore all day will be stripped from your wet, (often) blistered, cold feet, and roasted over a slow-burning fire (the drizzle keeps fires from blazing). The third pair you were saving for the sleeping bag are in your boots or tennis shoes getting wet. Remember, it's still drizzling. By the time you crawl into your sleeping bag, you will still be wearing one wet pair of socks and you may (if you are lucky) have one side of the other two pairs dry. (While one side dries next to the flame, the other side is being drizzled upon.) Thus you go to bed miserable, cold, and sockless. And the next day you put on wet socks. Therefore, always take a pair that remains with your sleeping bag—in fact, roll them up with the sleeping bag. The minimum number of pairs of socks recommended in drizzle country is five.

The Thirteen Essentials

The thirteen essentials are the things you should take on every trip no matter how brief the excursion.

Water
Always carry a minimum of two quarts of water for a hike of eight hours or longer. This is insurance in case the water is either contaminated or not available in the area you visit.

Knife
Every woodswoman should have her own knife. Just because your partner has one doesn't mean it will be available to you in an emergency.

There are many types of knives. The two favorites are the Buck knife and the Swiss Army knife. The Buck knife is a single blade which can be honed to a twenty-weight paper edge. Beautiful and symmetrical, it lasts forever and costs accordingly. The Swiss Army knife can vary from one or two simple blades to a multitude of accessories including a saw, tweezers, scissors, and can opener. Because knives come in all sizes, costs, and services, borrow one for your first few trips until you've discovered which functions best for you.

Maps
Whenever entering the backcountry, carry the necessary maps. Every member of the party should have copies of the maps being used and know how to read them. They should be carried at all times.

Compass
Like maps, every member of the party should have her own compass and know how to use it. Knowing where you are is the responsibility of each member of the group.

Matches

Always ensure that some of your matches are waterproofed. Keep several sets in different locations in your gear. If one place gets soaking wet or one set of matches is lost, another set will be on hand. As a final precaution, one set of matches can be coated with wax to keep them dry even if all the other gear gets wet. In an emergency, you can peel the wax off the head of the match. The wax will add fuel to the burning matchstick and cause the flame to last longer.

Candle

Candles provide a continuous flame for much longer periods than a match. In a drizzle or downpour, the candle flame can dry enough kindling to ignite larger pieces of wood.

If you trip has been cursed with ten days of constant rainfall, dry wood will be very difficult to find. However, in a constant, even misty rainfall, semidry kindling can be ignited with the use of a candle. Brown, dead lodgepole pine needles will ignite even when soaking so long as they are still attached to the branch.

A candle can fill in for a flashlight in an emergency. Candles are often used to provide that bit of psychological warmth in lieu of a campfire in heavily used areas.

Flashlight

Flashlights are good for emergency situations as well as for convenience once the shadows deepen. They can be used to find a route at night in an emergency and for signals.

Large Plastic Tarp

A large, sturdy plastic (waterproof) tarp can supply instant protection for you and your gear during a storm. It is not just for emergencies but can be used every day as a groundcover or shelter.

Some outdoorswomen use a space blanket instead of a tarp. Space blankets are lined with an aluminum substance on one side. When placed with the reflective side up in a tent or under a sleeping bag, body heat is reflected back to the user rather than letting it be drawn off by the cold ground. Space blankets are usually more expensive, bulkier, and sometimes heavier than tarps.

Extra Clothing
Always plan clothing for lower temperatures than one might expect. Carry a jacket even on short day trips away from basecamp. Even during the summer your wanderings could easily take you up to a ridgeline where a sudden snowstorm could catch you unprepared.

Extra Food
Like clothing, take more food than you'll need. The extra food should be of the high-energy variety. Good trail and emergency snacks can include dried fruits, candy, and cookies. A special candy composed of glucose is distributed under the brand of Kendal and comes in mint and butterscotch flavors. It is sold in mountaineering stores and is probably the haute cuisine of trail candies. Since glucose is a simpler sugar than sucrose (table sugar) it is easier to digest.

Cooking Cup
Getting drinks and eating is infinitely easier with some kind of receptacle. The Sierra cup, or one like it, is a favorite because the handle doesn't conduct heat from the cup to your hand and direct flame will not destroy the cup. If you have hypothermia and, no cook kit, drinking water heated over a fire in your cooking cup can save your life by instantly warming your insides.

First Aid Kit
Purchasing a standard first aid kit is not recommended. They are usually heavy, bulky, and not packaged to meet individual needs. Instead, assemble your own for the type of emergencies you may encounter. For example, you don't need a snakebite kit unless you're in snake country. See the first aid checklist at the end of this chapter for assistance.

Sunglasses
Sunglasses are an important and easy to overlook item. In

country where there is direct and reflective sunlight, such as from snow, ice, and water, your eyes can become damaged from excessive exposure. Some people get headaches from bright sunlight. If you are frequently in such areas, the purchase of a good pair of mountaineering sunglasses is worth the investment. Most will have a rating which shows how much visible light they allow to penetrate. Often they are impact resistant and include side protectors to prevent stray glare. Less precision sunglasses are fine for the casual outdoorswoman, providing they offer protection over fashion.

In Benediction of the Bandanna

On your list of thirteen essentials, add another: the bandanna. Don't leave home without it. For backpacking, there's no item worth praising more than the common, cotton, cowboy bandanna.

A bandanna is lightweight, inexpensive, and colorful. Just for pure aesthetics, it provides a little color to your neck or hat. But it has a more functional role than appearance.

1. Hot? Take off your bandanna and dip it into the cool stream. Squeeze or rub the cool water along your hot face and neck. When you resume hiking, redip the bandanna and frequently dampen and cool the hot spots as you walk along. Aaah. Redip the bandanna whenever you come to a new stream crossing.

2. Insects? Bandanna to the rescue. As you hike or sit, keep the bandanna rhythmically moving, killing or brushing away the barrages of pesky flies or mosquitoes. Like a rolled-up towel, the snap of a bandanna will demolish a bothersome horsefly or bee.

3. No shade? The bandanna will be your hat. Or your shade under the hat. When dampened, the bandanna can be a cool hat. One wet bandanna placed over the head, with another twisted bandanna tied around the head, will provide a silly-looking but very cool hat. If your real hat is providing shade but not much coolness, place the damp bandanna under your hat for awhile.

4. Wounded? Grab a clean bandanna and apply pressure to

the bleeding area. Or use the bandanna as a bandage. Or better yet, use one bandanna as a bandage, the other to tie it on with. When faced with such a horror as possible loss of limb due to severe bleeding, the bandanna will rush to the rescue as a top-rate tourniquet.

5. No rope? When you're looking for a short piece of rope, the rolled bandanna will become a sturdy helper that can easily be tied into knots and loops.

6. Runny nose? Bloody nose? Our bandanna serves well as a handerchief for both problems. It can be easily rinsed, dried, and reused.

7. Hot pots? A folded bandanna becomes a potholder.

8. Dirty pots? A bandanna becomes a wash rag.

9. Dirty body? A bandanna becomes a washcloth or towel.

10. Unexpected menstruation? The bandanna can get you through.

11. Cold? On a cold night, snuggle into your warm sleeping bag, put on your warm, wool hat, and wrap your bandanna around your neck to keep the night chills from creeping into the bag with you.

12. Perspiring? When water is dripping into your eyes, the bandanna can become your windshield wiper. Or it can be worn in a rolled position around your forehead, knotted in the back Indian-style, to keep the sweat from dribbling down your nose.

13. Wind, dust, smoke, or hail storms? Worn bandit-style, the bandanna will protect your face.

Bandannas come in a variety of colors and designs, although there is a traditional design of red or blue with a white and black background. Usually bandannas are made of cotton and come in two different sizes. Just about every sporting goods store, drugstore, western store, mountaineering store, discount store, or department store carry bandannas in their clothing or accessories sections.

Other important items are an extra pair of shoelaces, sanitary napkins or tampons, toilet paper, salt, water purifying chemicals, needle and thread, insect repellent, rope, medicine, moleskin, and sunscreen.

Use the following checklist when preparing for your trip. Specialized endeavors require their own list.

Checklist
bandanna
hat
headnet (mosquito country)
boots
socks
extra shoelaces
camp-wading shoes
down booties or sleeping socks
T-shirt
halter top or bathing suit
long-sleeved shirt (cotton)
long-sleeved shirt (wool)
down vest
sweater
jacket
pants and shorts
belt
underwear
gloves
poncho
rain chaps
gaiters
tarp or tent
sleeping bag and liner
ground cloth
foam pad or air mattress (mattress patching kit)
nylon cord or heavy twine
rope
large plastic trash bag
maps
compass
trail guidebook
whistle
flare
wilderness permit
knife
matches (waterproofed)
candle

can opener
cup
water bottle
collapsible water jug
cook kit, grate, spoons
stove and fuel
scouring pad
biodegradable soap (all purpose)
small plastic bags
food and beverages
water
salt, sugar, other condiments
water purification chemicals
sunglasses
glasses, contact lenses, and cleaner
watch
sunscreen with PABA
ChapStick or lip ice
insect repellent
towel and wash cloth
comb or brush
toothbrush and toothpaste
napkins or tampons
toilet paper
trowel
sewing kit
safety pins
flashlight
bear bell(s) (in Grizzly country)
fishing tackle and license
camera equipment
books
musical instruments
pencil and paper
binoculars
ice ax
walking stick
backpack (!)
bunji cord/attaching straps

First Aid Kit

prescription medicine
antiseptic (iodine soap, alcohol, peroxide)
aspirin, codeine, or other painkiller
Band-Aids
sterile gauze pads
adhesive tape
elastic bandage
bandanna or triangular bandage
tweezers
snakebite kit
medical care manual (first aid or mountaineering)
moleskin or footslips

For extended trips include
sleeping medications
antibiotics
antihistamine
stimulant (caffeine)
laxative
antacid
calamine lotion
antidiarrheal agents
antinauseants
vaginal suppositories

EQUIPMENT QUESTIONS

Before you pack your backpack, ask yourself the following questions: Do I absolutely need it? How much does it weigh? How can I reduce its weight? What will I leave behind if I take this? How much does it cost? Is there anything I can use as a substitute that is cheaper, lighter and/or more effective? Is there another piece of gear I'm already taking that can function in its place? Is there some way I can package this to make it lighter? What could happen if I don't take this? What is the likelihood of this happening?

3

Physical Fitness

WILDERNESS ACTIVITIES ARE among the most demanding physical efforts. Unless you enjoy being confined to car camping or depending on a professional outfitter to boat you down a river or provide horses to haul you up the mountains, you need endurance to keep going for long distances and substantial muscle strength to pull up switchbacks, balance through boulder fields, or steady an oar in a twenty thousand cubic feet per second rapid.

Most excercise programs for women are too easy and stress looks over strength. In the rush to imitate the *Playboy* bunny, the upper part of the female body (other than the decolleté) has atrophied. Most health spas and gyms automatically guide women to the bench press, assuming their primary concern is their bust line. Running programs, while less obvious, have them schlepping around for six weeks doing fast walks when they could be running a mile. Where patronage stops and genuine concern for women begins is hard to determine. The underlying sentiment of most women's programs is that strength is only attractive in women if carefully concealed in an aura of softness.

Strength is attractive in both sexes. Female body builders such as Bridget Gibbons, the World Amateur Body Builders' Association Miss World, are startlingly beautiful. Of course, there's beauty in knowing you can hike fourteen miles shouldering a heavy pack or telemark through winter's powder with the sureness of an arctic fox.

Outdoors women need exercise programs aimed less at weight watching and bust building than at exchanging fat for muscle. The fitness program presented in this chapter will enable you to build the endurance and muscle power necessary for outdoor activities. It can be adjusted to fit the seriousness of your backcountry activities. Unless you are strong, under thirty, and constantly active, you'll need some fitness program. Minimum training is outlined, and you can build from there.

There are two kinds of strength, requiring two kinds of training. Moving long distances requires endurance. Calories are converted into energy in the mitochondria of the muscle cells. These microscopic heating plants keep you going mile after mile. Endurance depends on the ability of the body to provide oxygen for this process. The system that brings oxygen through the lungs and blood to the mitochondria is the aerobic system. Like distance runners, wilderness users rely heavily on their aerobic systems.

Sheer explosive muscle power comes from two energy systems which operate without oxygen. Hence, they are called anaerobic (without oxygen). The first (ATP-PC) comes into play in violent bursts of energy usually under 15 seconds but sometimes as much as 90 seconds. The second system (lactic acid) is used for intense exercise from 1½ minutes to 3 minutes. This system also helps refuel the first. The energy capacity of both is very small and is used almost as quickly as it is produced. In general, women have about one-half the anaerobic energy reserves of men. Both of these energy systems use the oxygen system for regeneration. For this reason, even if you're involved only in sports which require intense strength, you still need to develop your aerobics.

Developing the aerobic or endurance system and the anaerobic or power system requires two different training methods. The relative importance of the programs varies with your favorite wilderness transportation, but, aerobics are the most important for wilderness aficionados.

Fat and the Outdoorswoman

The average women in the United States has 9 to 13 percent more fat than her male counterpart. Young adult women carry from 21.9 to 29.8 percent of their total body weight in the form of fat. The average young adult man has between 10.9 and 22.3 percent body fat.

Fat increases the energy cost of any task that involves lifting your body, which includes just about every wilderness activity. The more fat you carry, the harder you must work to get up to that ridge line. Fat not only taxes the system each time you lift your legs or perform other work, but puts extra stress on your heart.

Trading fat for muscle is vital for wilderness activities not only because muscle moves the body, but because the conversion of all energy (the burning of calories) takes place in the muscle cells. A women who carries 13 percent more fat than a male partner operates at 13 percent less oxygen capacity since fat cells do not aid in the use of oxygen. She operates at 13 percent less anaerobic capacity for the same reason. When it comes to work performance, extra fat is like a double mortgage.

The only proven benefits of fat in the wilderness are longer survival during prolonged fasting, buoyancy when swimming since fat is lighter than muscle and water, and insulation in extreme cold. (1) These pluses are marginal at best when weighed against the disadvantages.

Women's greater fat content has such a great impact on their ability to exert energy that figures comparing the oxygen capacity of women and men are often adjusted to take this into account—like a golfer's handicap. This nonworking tissue, in addition to underdeveloped upper body muscles, is the reason most women cannot lift their own weight, as in pull-ups or push-ups. This handicap is of little consequence in a living room or behind a desk, but can create despair when sedentary women take to the outdoors with male partners. Unless you are more athletic and slimmer than the average woman in the United States, you are going to trail behind the average male, not because you're less determined, but because you have to work harder to accomplish the same results.

Some people say that the breasts and other areas of the female anatomy (presumably the hips and thighs) require women to carry more fat than men. The beer belly, however, is rarely given as a reason why men should not do well in a stressful environment. That the breasts are a functional part of being female is hardly a matter for debate, but certainly they do not account for a 13 percent difference.

A greater proportion of fat to body weight is not an obligatory part of being female, says Dr. Sarah A. Nunneley of the United States Air Force School of Aerospace Medicine. In the days when women were constantly pregnant, it may have served to maintain the necessary food supply. In fact, there is speculation that women who reduce their percentage of body fat too much cannot become pregnent.

In other cultures, there are dramatic departures from the norm in the United States. In the Manus of the Admiralty Islands, both women and men have the same broad shoulders, heavily muscled limbs, and little fat beneath the skin. (2) In Bali, according to anthropologist Geoffrey Gorer, women and men have little to no difference in build. Among many Oriental peoples, the sexes show little difference in body fat.

Although the genetic makeup of the sexes may differ from people to people, the soft, yielding, female body is probably less a result of biology than habit. Feminine fat is largely a result rather than a cause of women's more sedentary habits in the United States. Marathoner Bill Emmerton of Australia was shocked by the poor fitness of many women in the United States. In his home country and in Europe, "Women ran, swam, bicycled or at least walked . . . if only because there were not as many automobiles." (3) Indeed, among distance runners, the female-male difference in fat content is much smaller than in the general population.

Aerobics

Many of the benefits of aerobic or endurance training take place in the cells. The amount of oxygen the body can use for energy production is partially determined by the volume of blood circulating in the body. The number of red blood cells, which carry the hemoglobin, which in turn carries the oxygen, increase as the volume of blood increases. The percentage of red blood cells also increases per unit of blood as you get in better shape. Athletes have about 45 to 50 percent red blood cells in a hundred milliliters of blood, while non-athletes have about 26 to 27 percent.

The importance of the aerobic system to athletic performance is illustrated by the practice of blood doping. In blood doping, the blood is withdrawn and the red blood cells are extracted and put into cold storage while the plasma is reinjected. It is hoped that the body will regenerate the lost red blood cells in the three to four weeks before competition. The day before competition, the stored red blood cells are mainlined back into the body in anticipation that the increase will give the athlete an edge in oxygen carrying capacity. Studies show that the supercharged athletes do indeed perform better. (4)

Women are at a disadvantage in the aerobic system not only because of fat, but because they have fewer red blood cells per unit than men. Coupled with these obstacles is that, even with training, it appears the number and size of the mitochondria in the muscle cells and the concentration of important enzymes involved in oxygen use do not increase as much in women as in men who train similarly. (5)

In spite of the drawbacks women encounter in aerobics, they are not great enough to prevent impressive gains in endurance in short periods of time. Furthermore, research regarding the female capacity for strength and endurance was generally neglected until the mid-1970s. Some studies have produced misleading results, since sedentary women were matched against active men and the women were naturally found wanting.

The sedentary woman (as well as the sedentary man) has one immediate benefit when starting an aerobic training program. The results will be dramatic and immediate. The worse shape you are in, the faster you will improve.

The law of diminishing returns seems to hold true in athletics as well as in economics. If you are already in good shape, then the results of your training program will not be so apparent. Once you reach a certain level of fitness, improving it to any extent seems to require a geometrical increase in effort.

A study conducted by a team of Japanese scientists at the University of Tokyo showed that an increase of 16 to 17 percent in maximum oxygen uptake can be achieved in eight weeks in two sessions per week at ten minutes per session. The women measured were between 18 and 20 years old and inactive. The team also concluded that work capacity (maximal oxygen uptake) is more due to the *intensity* than the frequency of the workout. However, they noted, training frequency apparently improved the efficiency of the heart, especially when the women did not work to maximum capacity. In other words, working hard for ten minutes will increase the power of your aerobic system—more air will get to more muscle cells faster producing more energy. If you work frequently, say for twenty minutes per session, but not so hard, your lungs and heart will eventually begin to deliver more oxygen and blood to the tissue without as much work.

This means is that for a stopgap program, you can prepare for a trip two months ahead of time and greatly improve your performance and fun with as little as two workouts a week for ten minutes. However, if you plan to cover more than a few comfortable miles a day, it is wise to train three to four times per week for twenty minutes each session. This way you'll improve not only your ability to handle the short stretches but miles of steady exercise.

The object of aerobic training is to keep your heart rate constantly above its resting rate. Running, skipping rope, cycling, and swimming make this easy since the motion is constant. Intermittent sports such as golf and doubles in tennis don't work well.

Skill in various activities is most rapidly acquired by training methods which most nearly duplicate the activity itself. For example, hikers and skiers should run, jog, or skip rope. Women new to boating should swim since primarily the upper body is used in swimming as it is in boating, and women are disproportionately weak above the waist. However, boaters are in danger of using too little of their lower bodies. Boaters need to go out of their way to exercise the lower body, unless they plan to do a lot of portages.

Boater or not, if you decide to swim for aerobics, do the crawl in a steady lap-after-lap rhythm or you won't be working anything but your sinuses. Swimming, however, can give a deceptive measure of fitness because the fat that floats in the water drags when out of water.

Cycling, both stationary and mobile, is a good choice for wilderness training since it exercises the leg muscles through a great range of positions, from fully extended to almost a 45 degree angle. Because stationary cycling allows you to adjust the pressure exerted, it is easier to keep your pulse at a constant rate. Mobile cycling is more difficult to regulate, but is more fun. Cycling, as in other exercises which develop your legs, also strengthens the knees and ankles, thereby lessening your chances of injuries.

The values between these exercises are not great enough to justify staunch advocacy of one against the other. Use whichever you're most likely to pursue with regularity.

During training you need to determine if you're working hard enough to do any good. Getting in touch with your body is one method perhaps, but a more accurate way is to check your progress from time to time by taking your pulse immediately after you stop exercising. When you take your resting pulse make sure you actually resting. Even standing up can increase your pulse enough to scare you to the doctor's office.

Pulse points which are fairly easy to read are the radial artery in your wrist and the carotid artery on the side of your throat below the jaw. Don't press too hard on the carotid artery since you can cut off blood to the brain and maybe faint. Don't use the thumb to measure since you will register the peculiar flutter of two pulses, the one in your thumb and the one you're trying to measure.

Once you find the pulse, count for fifteen seconds and multiply by four to make a sixty-second reading. The more seconds that tick by, the less accurate your reading will be. Take the pulse for six seconds and add zero. This will give your heart even less chance to slow down.

The average pulse for most young untrained women and men is 60 to 80 beats per minute. Once you've started training, you should notice a drop in your resting pulse rate. This reflects your improved circulatory efficiency.

Your age and fitness level determine the level at which you should train. Find your maximum heart rate (the hardest your heart can work) by subtracting your age from 220. (The only way to find this out for sure is to have a stress electrocardiogram taken.) The maximum heart rate or pulse for most women is 200 beats per minute although it declines with age. If you are 25 that would make your maximum heart rate 195 beats per minute; if you're 40 it would be 180 and so forth.

Laurence E. Morehouse, an authority on physical fitness, advises beginners to train at 60 percent of their maximum heart rate, although results can be achieved with less. You can adjust this to how you feel. Keep this up for about eight weeks, then move to a 70 percent level for the next eight weeks, and to a top level of 80 percent. As you get in shape your biological age will, in effect, drop. The increase in your heart rate while working will diminish, and you'll have to work harder to reach the 80 percent goal. In highly trained endurance athletes the resting heart rate is about 40 to 55 beats per minute. The reason your heart rate drops, in spite of the fact you're working harder, is because you've increased the amount of blood pumped by the heart per stroke per minute. Some marathon runners insist that the only way to really improve strength is to keep the heart pumping at 80 percent of its maximum for the duration of the exercise. This is hard to do, as you'll soon discover. This is perhaps the elusive difference between jogging and running. Even if you're slugging along at a 15 minute mile, you're running if your heart is pounding away at 80 percent of its maximum. You might not look like you're running but, as far as your body is concerned, you are.

If you are over 30 and sedentary and smoke, you should not launch into a high intensity program. Start at the low or moderate level. If you can get to a higher rung faster, do so. You, better than anyone else, know what you can do. See a doctor, preferably one who is sympathetic to women and knowledgeable about sports physiology, if you have any doubts. This is especially so if you have a history or any indication of heart trouble, arthritis, eye problems, or other ailments which could be aggravated by endurance training. Young people in their early 20's also should see a competent doctor, since they probably have not bothered with yearly checkups and may therefore have no idea what their bodies have been doing. Anyone who sees a doctor should remember that the more she knows about herself, the more good a doctor can do. You share responsibility for correct diagnosis and treatment.

No one should do strenuous exercise such as running stairs or hills until well on the road to good physical fitness. The chances of getting hurt are great enough to prevent that trip to the wilderness. In addition, irreparable damage can occur. A friend with tendonitis got that way because she hiked 15 miles with a 40-pound pack her very first time on the trail. Another friend developed the same problem after he ran 6 miles the first time he put on a pair of track shoes. Football injuries are high at the beginning of the season because many athletes don't trouble with a preseason conditioning program. This is another very good reason to measure your wilderness partners carefully before you're thirty miles out there. Don't go with people who may try to push you beyond your limits.

Smokers probably already know that smoke replaces the oxygen molecules in the blood stream with carbon monoxide molecules. When you smoke, you're obstructing the oxygen delivery system and letting less oxygen get to your muscles. When you're in the backcountry, you probably smoke less. This is good for two reasons: one, since the effects of smoking are cumulative, the less you smoke, the better; and two, because the immediate negative effects of smoking can be lessened if you stop 24 hours before you hit the trail. One woman said her most heroic act was not to climb Mt. McKinley or run Lava

Falls on the Colorado River, but to stop smoking. Those who are less heroic, or more addicted, can at least improve their performance by well-timed abstinance.

The Anaerobic System

As mentioned previously, women do not have as much gross muscle power as men. In one test group, after a ten-week training program, the upper body strength of the men was 50 percent higher than the women. Their lower body strength was 25 percent higher. (6) Much of this disparity is probably the result of what women think they should be able to do. The impact of learning on human behavior is so great that it is often very nearly impossible to separate innate abilities from socially determined ones.

Some suggest that if physical fitness was sought equally by both sexes, there would only be a 5 percent difference in strength. (7) Presently, the difference in top athletes is not more than 10 to 15 percent.

Both anaerobic systems have a small energy capacity that is used almost as quickly as it is produced. The ATP-PC system provides violent bursts of energy, usually under fifteen seconds long but sometimes as long as ninety seconds. It can be partially restored by about three minutes of rest; full restoration requires twenty to thirty minutes of rest.

The lactic acid system is used for intense exercise of one and a half to three minutes. It also helps refuel the first, because it restores the phosphahgens lost from the ATP-PC system during intense exercise. The lactic acid system converts muscle sugar to energy without oxygen, leaving the waste product of lactic acid. This lactic acid produces muscle fatigue.

Both these energy systems use oxygen for regeneration. So even if you're involved only in sports requiring intense strength, you need to develop your aerobics. For example, the more efficiently your oxygen system works, the better it will get rid of lactic acid, thus minimizing muscle fatigue.

Isometric exercises, the movement of muscle against fixed objects, are not recommended because the strength gained is limited to that part of the muscle used in the position in which the exercise is done. (8)

Weight training programs for women emphasize that muscle enlargement (hypertrophy) is not nearly as great in women as it is in men. Actually, much depends on the amount of the male sex hormone testosterone in your system. Both sexes have it, and the amount varies greatly from one person to the next. Some women will develop larger muscles than others. Some may even develop muscles like a man's. Some muscles, like biceps and pectorals, will come closer to the size of a man's than others like shoulders (deltoids) and upper back and neck (trapezius). However to look like a power lifter, you have to train like one, putting most of your waking hours into that goal. A more likely problem is finding the time and motivation to do the minimum amount of weight training.

Weight training presents several problems. The biggest one is finding weights. Kathryn Lance, in her book *Getting Strong*, has developed a system using plastic bottles, brooms, and other household items as weights. Other sources are health clubs, the YWCA, a nearby college, a friend, and buying your own. Some lifters say it costs less to invest in a beginner's set of dumbbells and barbells than to join a club, and you won't have to wait in line during weekend and afterwork rush hours.

There are three basic weight training apparatuses: free weights, barbells and dumbbells; the Nautilus system, a series of weights and pulleys affixed to machines; and the Universal system, a combination of weight machines and free weights. Some believe that the Nautilus system is superior for women since, as you do not pick up the weights with your hands, you don't need a strong grip, which is an obstacle for sedentary women. Ironically, the Nautilus was developed by Arthur Jones, who loves women so much that he says every man should own at least four of them. Although much has been said pro and con about all three systems, excellent results can be had with any of them.

You may feel odd, even intimidated, on first entering the weight room. The odor of machismo is at its most pungent as tortured souls rack their bodies and cry out. You will probably feel even worse when you discover how pitifully weak you are above the waist. The ratio between arm and leg strength in women is about three to one; in men it is about two to one.

If you are a beginner and not above a little functional opportunism, you are at an advantage if you want some help. Most men (and women, too) love to showboat, and many will assume that a woman doesn't know what she's doing. You won't be ignored, it is more likely you will receive a lot of unsolicited advice, especially if you look delicate. Take this for what it is—patronage mixed with a quaint and not unattractive degree of chivalry. Once you know what you're doing, it will be obvious, and accept or reject advice depending on the source.

Before beginning a weightlifting program, read one of the better books on the topic. *Especially for Women* by Ellington Darden and *Starbodies* by Franco and Anita Columbu offer comprehensive training programs. *Starbodies* uses the Universal and free weight system, while *Especially for Women* uses the Nautilus. However, the exercises in each book are adaptable to any weight training equipment. Use either these two books or others on the topic for good illustrations of how to do specific exercises. However, rather than following to the letter the programs in these books, adopt the ones most useful for your self-designed program.

Although everyone agrees that you should work out at approximately the same time of day, there is much debate over how many repetitions, how much weight, and how many sets of each exercise. One theory is that light weights with twelve repetitions per exercise done in a series of three sets per exercise is the best way to build muscle endurance with less emphasis on brute strength. On the other end of the spectrum is the theory of lifting the most you can for a minimum of eight repetitions with only one set per exercise. Once you can do twelve exercises in good form, increase the weight. This should build gross strength faster. Neither theory has been proven. Interestingly, the first is the one most often recommended for women, because it is the "slim and trim" approach.

Even though the jury's still out, the second seems preferable for building anaerobic strength. In wilderness activities, your anaerobic systems is called on when you need a lot of power quickly. If you have to climb a tree to get away from a moose or grizzly, you'll want to do so fast. Also, the maximum weight, minimum set approach is faster, You shouldn't need to spend more than about twenty minutes in the weight room.

About 60 percent of your workout should be devoted to your upper body, particularly if your aerobic program doesn't include swimming. This is to make up for the disparity between upper and lower body strength. If you swim for aerobics, devote about 40 percent of your anaerobic program to your upper body. Also consider your normal activities. If you are a telephone linewoman, you will probably be pretty strong above the waist. The goal is total body strength with special emphasis on the parts that do the most work. Upper body strength is important if you want to get past day hiking and into the backcountry. You will need this strength to carry a pack, split logs, scramble up boulder fields, or if you encounter an emergency and have to carry someone out.

Trial and error is the best way to find out how much weight to lift. Don't be surprised if at first you cannot lift more than ten pounds with your arms, chest, and shoulder muscles, unless you already actively use those muscles. Work at each exercise until you are exhausted, but make sure you are still doing the exercise in the right form during the last repetition. Stay with the same amount of weight until you can do the exercise twelve times in good form without exhaustion.

The muscle groups should be worked from the largest to the smallest so you won't tire before you are finished. A workout should consist of approximately twelve exercises with emphasis on the upper body. Muscle groups should be exercised in the following order:

1. hips, back, and buttocks (external obliques, erector spinae and gluteus maximus)
2. abdominals
3. thighs and hamstrings (quadriceps and biceps femoris)
4. calves and shins (gastrocnemius and anterior tibialis)
5. chest (pictorals)
6. shoulders (deltoids)
7. underarm and back (lattissimus dorsi)
8. neck and back (trapezius)
9. back arm (tricep)

10. front arm (bicep)
11. wrist and forearm
12. ankles

The chart shows which exercises are best for each muscle group. All the exercises work more than just one muscle, which makes it easy to kill two, three, or even four birds with one stone. Some exercises are exclusive to the Nautilus system, while others are exclusive to the Universal system. Most can be duplicated by analyzing the muscle groups they work. Some do not use weights at all but are included because they are the best or only way to work a particular muscle.

Again, determine the muscle groups you need to exercise. The following program is aimed at the backpacker. If rock climbing, kayaking, cross-country skiing, and rafting are part of your wilderness program, you may want to add, subtract, or place more emphasis on specific muscle groups.

1. hips, back, and buttocks (one or two exercises) Many exercises will vicariously work these muscles while working others.
2. abdominals (one exercise) Same as above.
3. thighs and hamstrings (two or three exercises)
4. knees and ankles (one exercise) Almost all exercises which strengthen legs will work on knees and ankles too.
5. pectorals (two or three exercises)
6. trapezius (two or three exercises)
7. latissimus dorsi (two or three exercises)
8. triceps (one exercise)
9. biceps (one exercise)

When you weight train, expect sore muscles. The exercise will hurt, your heart rate will increase, and your breath will come quickly. These are all signs that you're causing enough stress to do some good. Muscle soreness is generally thought to be caused by the stretching of the connective tissue, ligaments and tendons, rather than an actual tearing of the muscle itself. Muscle tears are possible and connote an injury, not progress. At no time should the hurt be debilitating. When first starting you will indeed be very sore but this lessens with practice. You should not be immobilized. Do not combine weight training with aerobic exercise because in weight training the goal is to

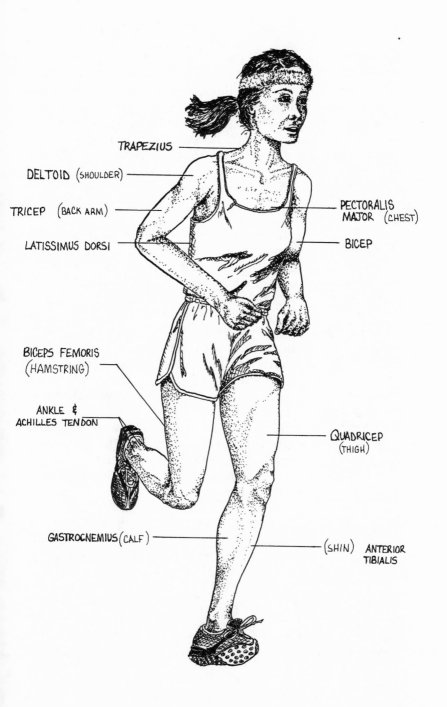

TRAPEZIUS

DELTOID (SHOULDER)

TRICEP (BACK ARM)

LATISSIMUS DORSI

PECTORALIS MAJOR (CHEST)

BICEP

BICEPS FEMORIS (HAMSTRING)

ANKLE & ACHILLES TENDON

QUADRICEP (THIGH)

GASTROCNEMIUS (CALF)

(SHIN) ANTERIOR TIBIALIS

work each muscle to short-term exhaustion. Alternate days or do both on the same day but at different times. Most weight training coaches agree on a three day per week schedule. This will produce gains in strength without risking chronic fatigue. Overtraining or not allowing day-to-day or set-to-set recovery does more harm than good. It takes about 48 hours for the muscles and their support system to recuperate from a training session.

Your Total Program

If you make a living outdoors, you won't have to concentrate on the training program as much as the occasional hiker will. If your work is seasonal, during the season train for maintenance of strength and endurance with weekly or twice-weekly workouts. This reduces the risk of injury, yet you'll avoid the chronic fatigue of overtraining.

During high intensity workouts, work hard but don't be ridiculous. Don't measure yourself against others, especially men. Allow enough rest time for the body to rebuild and renew itself. Chronic fatigue and overwork won't make you a better outdoorswoman, but will make you old before your time like Dorothea Lange's Dust Bowl women.

Coaches insist that a warm-up session is essential for both anaerobic and aerobic exercise. The premise of the warm-up is that it prevents injury by priming the muscles and nerve endings for action. Blood is pumped to the muscle, thereby raising the muscle temperature. Increased heat in the muscle may aid in the muscle contraction. Stretching exercises increase the range of motion of those muscles, reducing the possibility of injury. One mountaineer has a permanently weak pectoral muscle because of the time he separated it from his breastbone. He had failed to warm up before a demanding aerial gymnastics program.

To warm up for weight training, do a few stretching exercises such as toe touches, sit-ups and (if you can) push-ups. Do enough to produce a flush and get the blood moving. Lightly exercise those muscles which you will use in your weight training. At all times, do the exercises in smooth, even motions. Don't jerk, and don't hold your breath. When you do heavy exercise, it's extremely important to breathe. If you hold your breath while pressing 100 pounds, you might pop a blood vessel!

The warm down or cooling off period is very important, especially in aerobic exercise. In both aerobic and anaerobic exercise, the lactic acid system will be spurting its waste into your system. Some experts also believe that during exercise the blood rushes away from the core of the body to the areas being exercised. If you collapse right after a heavy workout, you allow the lactic acid to stay in the muscle and encourage a great surge of blood back to the internal organs. The consequence is fatigue from the lactic acid system and cramps from the surge. After you run, swim, cycle, or lift weights, a period of light exercise is in order. Let your pulse come back to about 40 percent of normal. This will take longer the more out of shape you are. This also applies when you are in the backcountry. After you've done all that work, don't just flop down in camp. If you're coming out, don't just jump in the car and drive 300 miles home. Stop, get out, walk around, stretch for a few minutes. If you don't, your muscles will freeze up like a dried-out master cylinder. Morning in camp will find you full of aches and pains. The light exercise disperses the lactic acid into the waste system and forces the blood to enter the internal organs more slowly.

Once you get involved in weight training, you may actually look forward to the twenty minutes of pumping iron. On the other hand, you may not like it at all but look forward to your swimming or running. It's possible that you won't especially like either, although many wilderness users enjoy activity for its own sake. If you hate the exercise but love the scenery of the outdoors, don't despair. You don't have to feel a rush when you work with weights. You don't have to get high when you run. You don't have to become more potent, more seductive, more intelligent, less irritable, or less nervous, because you're involved in physical fitness. What will happen is that if you work hard at becoming stronger, you'll have a lot more fun in the backcountry.

4

Great Expectations

SO YOU ARE ready to go get 'em. Maybe it's your very first outing or the first one of the season. For preparation, you've been running for lunch rather than eating it. You have diligently weight-trained. Maybe you've taken seven- or eight-mile hikes or sashayed around a swimming pool in a kayak.

But watch out for great expectations—delusions of grandeur. Unless you're Hannibal with all the aid and comfort 40,000 troops and elephants can muster, don't expect to cross the Pyrénées, or hike 13 miles and 2,000 feet upwards in new hiking boots. Recreational hiking is just that, recreation, not punishment.

For beginners, the rewards of overestimation are exhaustion, blisters the size of silver dollars, and secluded tears as you bring up the rear. The more experienced are likely to find that the trail they counted on disappeared in the fecund spring meadow or washed away with the snowmelt. Ah, reality bears little resemblence to reverie.

Who you take your first outing with and how well you plan it can mean the difference between a great experience and hanging up your walking shoes. That's why it's important to find out ahead of time how far your friends intend to go and what their trip objectives are. Novices, as well as experienced woodswomen, report that many men (as well as some women) will attempt to force the outing into a marathon. If you slow them down, you receive contempt or condescending concern for your welfare. If you keep up, they slap you on the back and tell you "you're a credit to your gender." An indication beforehand of how you'll fare on the trip is how much input you're permitted during in-trip preparation such as where, how many miles, how well traveled, and how many stream crossings. Remind them that you want to enjoy yourself, or that you expect to journey no more than seven miles a day. If they pooh-pooh your concerns, find someone else.

A male friend worked for a land management agency and loved the outdoor life. His wife of eight years didn't like hiking. She didn't like to perspire and didn't like to go too far. They tried backpacking when they were first married, and she refused to go again. It was suggested to him to try taking her on some short trails during a pleasant month of the year, and combine the trip with bird-watching, beautiful scenery, and wildflowers.

He took his wife on a short trail (five miles) with the promise of birdwatching and wildflowers. What he neglected to consider about the trail was that it was poorly marked with scratchy vegetation growing all over it. It was steep and completely downhill with a 2,000-foot elevation loss. There was no water until the last section, and being that time of year (from snowmelt to late June), the ticks were in force. The poor woman had a miserable time and swore never to hike again.

In a more successful case, a man planned to take his novice wife to the lovely and famous Teton National Park in Wyoming. The Park's trails are so crowded that reservations are required. They arrived at park headquarters at 8:15 A.M. The trail and campsite they wanted in the Tetons' Death Canyon was full, so the ranger said they had space in Granite Canyon, but that their campsite was 13 miles in with a 3,000-foot elevation gain. The wife, unaware of what 13 miles and 3,000 feet means, was willing to go. Wisely, the husband suggested they save that hike for another time. Instead, they drove around to the less popular, west side of the range where reservations weren't needed, found a lovely trail, and hiked a leisurely 3 miles through lush green country. She was sold and eventually graduated to much more difficult endeavors.

The purpose of the first outing is to have an enjoyable time. Attempt to make your first experiences pleasant ones. Do the same for beginners in your charge. Let the novices set the pace. If you're hiking in national parks and other places where campsites must be reserved, pick the easiest ones until you know your partner's capabilities. Since the novice has so little experience, you'll probably be a better judge of what she can do than she is.

On this topic Slim Woodruff comments, "The first overnighter should be short and in well-traveled areas and taken with an experienced companion. And pay attention to what they tell you! I took a young woman friend out over Thanksgiving because she wanted to learn to backpack. She decided on her own that she didn't need all the equipment I recommended. So she started out into the desert with one quart of water, no warm coat, no foam pad to sleep on, and I have no idea what else she left behind. She hiked for twenty-six hours on that quart of water since the springs were dry, froze to death at night, and got terrible blisters because her boots were too small. She hated it, and we came back from the trip two days early.

"Once back at the car, she convinced herself that her problem lay in her heavy pack. She was all set to go back out with only what she thought she needed: a sleeping bag. She failed to convince me, and we car-camped for the rest of our vacation."

Experienced outdoorswomen have to watch out for complacency. Just because you've done it a thousand times, doesn't mean you don't need a checklist or that you don't need to plan ahead, as the following story shows.

It was December in California's San Rafael Wilderness, and I had debated whether or not to go on a five-day patrol of the Wilderness. December is the month of rains in California, and the sky seemed ominously threatening.

The other jobs at the ranger station were at a standstill, so I spontaneously decided to take the trip anyway. I wanted to finish some campfire cleanup and explore a dry canyon.

I hastily arranged a ride with another patrol person, threw together my gear, and crossed my fingers for no rain, since I was leaving behind my heavy tent and taking a lightweight plastic tarp instead.

Little did I realize how much else I'd really left behind. The first thing I noticed missing was my cup. Normally I drink and eat out of an aluminum Sierra cup. This trip I was to eat and drink out of a tin foil bag that once held a freeze-dried dinner. I washed this "cook kit" periodically.

I did remember matches, so I was able to start a fire conveniently. However, I had forgotten a spoon or fork to stir or eat my food with. I would have made a spoon out of wood with my knife, but the knife was still next to the kitchen sink where I'd left it.

I'm proud that I didn't cut myself on the metal can—the can I opened with a rock and a heavy, strong, semipointed stick. You know the can I'm talking about, the can of oysters I'd saved for my special last night meal . . . but I forgot the can opener.

Normally, it doesn't bother me to forget soap as backpacking is a dirty business anyway, but I would have appreciated a small bar on that trip after cleaning out the soot and ash from ten messy campfires.

But at least I had clean teeth as I'd remembered my toothpaste. Well, I did forget the toothbrush but that was easy to remedy—I just used my dirty fingers. My fingers were black because I had no soap to clean them with after I'd cleaned the campfires. But that's OK, since they say charcoal is good for the teeth.

I guess a flashlight really isn't all that important. I just stacked up an unusually high pile of firewood so I could write by firelight. Unfortunately, it was the shortest days of the year so it was dark by 5 P.M.

When I returned to the trailhead after my five-day adventure, I propped my pack against a rock and waited for my ride. Was he going to come at 2 or 3 P.M? Was I supposed to meet him here or at the other trailhead? That's funny. I don't usually forget such things.

Most of the time you can get by with just a sleeping bag and some food. As one alpine climber once said, "I'd rather turn back ten times too early, than once too late." Items such as first aid, extra clothing and food, maps and compass, and extra water in the desert seem to add unnecessary pounds until such time as you need them, then they're priceless, Slim says.

It seems elementary to say that the longer the trip, the heavier the load. However, many backpackers, especially women, occasionally don't carry enough food for the sake of saving weight. Sometimes running out of food happens even if you've allotted plenty for the time you plan to spend in the wilderness.

Victoria Montgomery, relates the time she and a partner ran out of food during a trek on Canada's Vancouver Island. They planned on taking seven to eight days on the fifty-mile trail. Instead, the trip stretched into ten days. By the time they realized they would run out of food, they were too far along to turn back.

"The trail resembled a training site for the Marines," she says. It was very muddy, sometimes two or three feet deep in the ooze. There were deep ravines with remnants of decayed bridges crossing them and numerous high creeks. It was also a rain forest. The trail was just plain dangerous, she says. In some places it ran beside the ocean and if you didn't gage your timing, you could get caught stranded during high tide. "We had to rope ourselves across rivers. The trail had severe, abrupt drops. We tumbled down small (five-foot) drops, slid down hillsides, and one day, when we were walking through a severe blow-down area, my partner slipped off a log and knocked himself out. One day we got totally lost and only made 1½ miles in about twelve hours."

On the fifth day, when they realized they would probably run out of food, they began to ration what they had. "We happened upon some people on the beach to whom a fisherman donated a 200-pound cod. They invited us to dinner. I ate and ate. It was heaven sent," she says.

Seldom will you find level terrain throughout a trip or even during one day of a trip. Some trips will be up and down, up and down. Others will be straight up all day or straight down.

Vicki comments that they mistakenly assumed that because the trail was near a major population center, it would be a good one. This assumption led them not to bother with a topographic map or compass. "We wouldn't have known how to read them anyway," she says. They also didn't check with locals about the condition of the trail. "We found out later that the RCMP (Royal Canadian Mounted Police) had helicopters out there all the time to rescue hikers who got stranded when the tide came in." The two ate a lot of salmonberries, mussels, some smelt, and huckleberries to stretch their food supply. "But our fishing rod broke and the streams were pretty well fished out," she says. "I'd sure hate to have to depend on living off nature after having a brush with being forced to do so."

Counting on catching enough fish or finding enough berries to make up for the food you left behind is foolish. Don't use a hike for dieting. Don't skimp on food. If the trip is long and the country rough, take extra.

After carefully choosing your companions and gear, familiarize yourself with topographic maps of the area, government regulations, climate and vegetation patterns, wildlife, and guidebooks of the area.

Remember the difference between linear miles and effort miles when deciding how far to travel. An effort mile is equal to one linear mile for every 500 feet of elevation gained. Then there's hiking miles versus backpacking miles. The average backpacker makes about seven miles a day. The average hiker, without a backpack, can easily double that figure. City and pastoral hikes and ski tours are generally on fairly level terrain with clearly marked trails, devoid of switchbacks, bugs, brush, rock outcroppings, downed timber, stream crossings, and other hazards. It's much easier to cover any of the these than genuine backcountry. Remember that, and allow for it, regardless of your experience or credentials.

Some people prefer an unhill grade to a downhill. This is because going up is not as hard on the knees and ankles, although it's certainly harder on your wind. Those who don't like downhill probably haven't figured out how to do it easily. Many hikers like downhill hiking because, not having to worry about getting their breath, they can sing, talk, and enjoy the scenery.

This downhill technique may not work for you, but it has for everyone who catches on. The theory is simple—let gravity do most of the work. Offer little resistance. This technique does require a trail. It won't work on boulders or other areas which require balance and delicate footwork.

On a well-cleared path, once you start downhill, develop a rhythm. Rather than stopping with each step, lean forward and take big strides, giving in at the knees. You will find yourself bouncing along the trail, almost at a run. At first, you may feel a little nauseous as the pack bounces slightly against your back in an annoying manner as you rhythmically leave the earth. (Incidentally, packs with waist straps are necessary for this kind of downhill hiking.) The feeling, similar to seasickness, leaves with a few minutes of practice.

This method not only gets you down in half the time, it also saves wear and tear on your legs, knees, feet, and ankles.

On the other hand, gravity will never help you climb a hill. Just getting enough air limits your speed. You can actually reach a point where you can't get enough oxygen for your muscles to function. This could be because you're out of condition, made the change in elevation too quickly, or simply are up too high to adjust readily.

When going uphill, it's better to be the tortoise than the hare. A steady pace that keeps your breathing rhythmic is better than the stop-and-rush technique of the hare. Because of the energy capacity of the aerobic system, you will last longer and experience less pain and fatigue if you take it slow and steady.

For hikers, the rest step is one way of keeping a steady pace. The rest-stepper brings the back foot past the other foot and slightly pauses when they are adjacent before placing it ahead. This step is also a psychological boon for getting up steep inclines.

On a long upward climbs, seldom look ahead. Instead try to enjoy the scenery and look back occasionally to savor the victories behind.

When you stop for a breather, it's better not to sit down. This just makes it harder to get going again. Resting your pack against a rock or tree while still wearing it will provide relief until your pulse comes back to normal.

Avoid overestimating your abilities the first time out. Besides the heaviness of your pack and the difficulty of the terrain, think about your destination. You're not headed for the comforts of home and the fireside warmly burning. Comfort in camp is entirely of your own making. When you arrive, you've got to consider where to put your tent, where to locate the kitchen, gathering firewood or getting that crusty stove to cooperate, finding the food in your pack, getting the water, cooking, then cleaning, then—finally—a sponge bath. Yes, getting there, even if you have a packstring which would shame the Budweiser Clydesdales, is only part of the effort. Save some energy for your destination. If you only have to take care of yourself, making camp can take about two hours. If you want to supplement dinner with fresh-caught trout, optimistically add at least two or three more hours.

Hopefully, backcountry is not a trial to see if you will physically survive. Your body will, but your attitude may not. How you remember your first trip may well determine whether it is your first or last adventure. Plan to enjoy it. Take what you like for comfort, and adjust miles accordingly.

Navigating

Navigating, specifically reading maps, is not something which comes easily to most women. Many do not want to be bothered with that mass of lines and routes. However, its mastery is the only way to be independent in the wilderness.

Navigation skills are not quite as important for those entering the highly developed and heavily used backcountry areas of the United States. Generally, these areas have guidebooks which show every step of the way. Some areas, such as Adirondack State Park, have a very refined trail system with white-blue- and red-painted blazes marking the main and side trails.

The eastern United States is far more trail-oriented than the west (except California), and the backcountry is generally more populated due to proximity to major population centers and a smaller backcountry land base. But the key in any backcountry area, comments Virginia Norris, former director of curriculum development for the National Outdoor Leadership School, is to go either to alternate spots or simply farther from the road-head. "This is particularly true in, say, the North Cascades of Washington where dense undergrowth and steep terrain make campsites few and far between," she says. "Tent cities occur in the Rockies, the Tetons, the Sawtooths, the Uintas—you name it and at some time of the summer the backcountry will be overpopulated in certain spots."

Often you can pull into a crowded camping area and be instantly alone by hiking slightly more than two or three miles. Sometimes a drop off a ridge line trail into a lake basin will bring you privacy if there are no obvious trails to the lake. Other times you can cross over to the other side of a ridge flanking a crowded valley and find nothing there but the birds and the bees.

Map reading is a necessary skill even if one visits only the more populous areas. Even well-marked trails pose the hazard of taking a wrong fork and getting lost. In addition, map reading makes the trip more fun as you correlate landmarks to the map and trace your progress. It's also part of the fun to know the names of various peaks and lakes.

The most heavily used areas are usually the most dramatically scenic. If a place is written up in a backpacking magazine, it is already heavily used. This rule applies even more so if the area makes it into a mass circulation publication such as newspapers and large circulation magazines. If you want to see the major wonders of the continent and don't mind being assigned a campsite and having to make reservations sometimes months in advance, these are the areas for you. However, if you want privacy, avoid them. There are literally hundreds of outstanding places to visit with little competition from others, if you are willing to learn the skills to take you there.

Maps

In the United States, by far the best maps are made by the United States Geological Survey (USGS). These usually come in three different scales. The smallest scale is the best for those on foot. Those traveling rivers and lakes can get by with the larger scale maps.

For the continental United States, the maps (from small to large scale) are 1:24,000 scale, 1 inch equals 2,000 feet. These are also identified as 7½-minute maps, which refers to minutes of longitude and latitude. These have contour intervals of 40 feet, although some of mountain areas are in 80-foot contour intervals.

The next size is 1:62,500, which 1 inch equals about 1 mile. These 15-minute maps usually have contour intervals of 80 feet, although if showing a very flat area, the intervals might be of 5 to 10 feet.

The largest scale is 1:250,000 where 1 inch equals about 4 miles. The intervals are 250 feet. These are practically useless for backcountry travel. For some areas, such as parts of Alaska, these may be all you can get.

The scale is slightly different for all three map sizes for Alaska, Puerto Rico, and Hawaii.

Getting the right maps may be as simple as walking into a mountaineering or sporting goods store and asking about the general vicinity. Another good source is a university library. If you don't have access to a good library, write to the USGS for the index of the state(s) you plan to visit. The index will tell you the names of the quadrangles. Each map in a series is called a "quadrangle." If using the 1:24,000 series, it will take several maps to route a trip, unless you are a slow mover or plan to go in circles. The index also shows how old the maps are and what series they come in. There is a nominal charge for maps ordered directly through the USGS.

Adjacent maps of the same quadrangle series are recorded in each map margin. Adjacent maps can then be combined to plan the trip. The map margin also indicates latitude and longitude (expressed in degrees and minutes), compass declination, miles to inches, and the name and date of the map.

The more recent the map, the better. Some of the USGS maps were made in the 1940s and haven't been updated. Consequently, trails are very likely not to be where they're supposed to be. The United States Forest Service and other government agencies often have updated maps which will show more recent trails. Since these maps do not usually show elevation, they're useful only as a supplement to the USGS maps.

The USGS maps stand out from the rest because of the contour intervals which show the shape and elevation of the terrain. They also show networks of streams and rivers, lakes, marshes, and other natural features, as well as man-made structures. When requesting maps, ask for the guide to topographic map symbols, which explains all those colors, dotted lines, hatches, and squares. Either memorize or carry the symbol guide with you on the outing.

A contour line represents an imaginary line of constant elevation on the earth's surface. A contour interval is the distance between two contour lines. To walk along a contour line would be to follow a level path, and by stepping off the contour, one must rise or descend. The terrain is steep where contour lines are close together. Where the lines are far apart, the slopes are gentle. If the slope is vertical as in cliffs, the contour lines will merge. Generally, every fifth contour line is heavier to make reading easier. At various points along these heavy lines, the elevation will be given.

To tell valleys from rises on a topographic map consult the elevation figures. In a valley the contour lines bend inwards as

The same section of land shown in actual relief and as expressed by contour lines. The back range of hills in the relief illustration is not shown in the contour illustration.

the elevation increases and forms a V. On a rise, the contour lines bend outward as the elevation increases. Still confused? Draw a line through the most pronounced bends in the contours. If the lowest elevation is convex, it's a rise. If the lowest elevation is concave, it's a valley. Another obvious indicator of a valley is a stream or river.

The red checkboard overlay with numbers assigned to each square depicts townships. Each numbered square represents a square mile, which can help you determine distance. Thirty-six squares make a township.

Another way to measure distance is to obtain a map wheel (map measure). This consists of a small wheel attached to an odometer. As you trace your route on the map, the odometer will register the distance.

Compasses

Compasses are always cited as necessities for wilderness travel. Consequently, as soon as family and friends learn of your interest in the backcountry, you'll probably receive a few as presents. Do not tuck it away in your backpack and forget about it. Learn how to use it.

Just about any compass points north, but unless you're experienced, you'll do better with a more sophisticated compass. Oddly, the simple compasses are sometimes recommended for beginners, the very people who need a good compass. While a sourdough may be able to float a needle in a pool of water to determine magnetic north, beginners need all the help they can get.

The outstanding feature of orienteering compasses is a transparent baseplate which can be laid on a map. These baseplates are ruled in inches and millimeters, and the compass housing can be rotated to match the dial points to true north.

Compass needles go haywire near magnetic objects such as belt buckles, cars, and rocks with iron deposits. If your needle spins this could be the problem. In areas of high iron ore deposit, such as lava formations, it is impossible to use a compass.

Compensating for compass declination, the difference between true north and magnetic north, is an essential skill. The compass needle will point to magnetic north. To navigate, you need to find true north.

In both the northeastern and northwestern United States, this difference can be as much as 20 degrees. In Alaska and the Hudson Bay area, it can be 30 degrees. At a 20-degree error, one can be thrown off the route by a mile in little more than three miles into the journey. (1)

The difference between true north and magnetic north increases as one nears the North and South Poles. These declination lines, which are measured from east to west, are gauged in degrees and waver erratically across the globe. The area in which true north and magnetic north are the same is termed the *agonic line* and wavers south from the North Pole through the Great Lakes area on down through Florida, then through Bolivia and Argentina. At points east of this line, the north end of the compass needle comes to rest at a point west of true north. At points west, the needle points in a direction east of true north.

If you don't have a compass on which you can set the declination, you can mark it permanently with a scratch. This works well until you travel far enough to have reached a different declination line—unlikely on foot, but possible if taking trips in different parts of the country.

Once you've set your declination, get your compass bearing. A bearing is measured in degrees calibrated clockwise around the edge of the compass (360 degrees). If your route is northeast, line up the north end of the compass needle with true north, and strike off in the northeast direction indicated on the compass. This all takes some practice, so learn it before you need it.

Sometimes the route the compass indicates is not the route that feels accurate. This innate sense of direction is not a sense of direction at all but a proven tendency of all people to circle. (2) Follow the compass, not your instinct. One woman almost got lost when the compass needle indicated which way was northeast—the direction she wanted to go—and she kept going north because it felt right. Being in thick timber, she couldn't see any landmarks. After wandering around for awhile, she started calling out to companions who were fishing at the lake she was trying to find. Fortunately, her error hadn't put her out of hearing distance. When they whistled back, she realized she was too far north—just like the compass read.

At night, locate true north using the North Star, Polaris. The two stars which form the outer edge of the cup of the Big Dipper point toward Polaris, which is brighter and larger than the other stars.

Some backpackers, skiers, and other land travelers always carry, but rarely use, a compass since trail systems are so well-marked and guidebooks have been written about many areas. Canoeists, however, may find them one of the most consulted

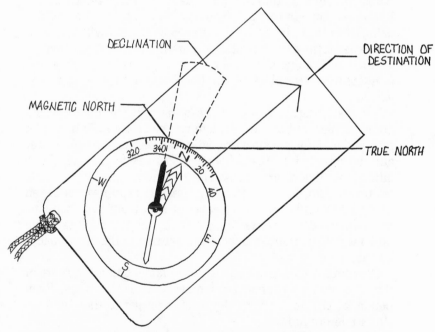

This compass is set to correct for a declination of sixteen degrees east of true north. Such a correction would be used, if west of the agonic line, when navigating from terrain to map. If navigating from map to terrain, reverse the setting; in this example, the declination would then be corrected by setting the compass at sixteen degrees east of magnetic north.

items in their gear. "This is especially true on large lakes and/or rainy weather when landmarks are not visible," says Virginia Bailey, a teacher and former Girl Scout camp director who has logged twenty years of canoe tripping in the Quetico-Superior lake country. "Most of the trails I've used are canoe 'trails,' and portages are the key points to locate. When canoeing lakes off the beaten track, we would often find a map-marked portage no longer usable, changed slightly in location, or even long since overgrown.

"Navigation maps were a necessity when traveling for days without seeing another person, in many places now one just needs to ask, 'Where is the next portage,'" she says.

Women are experts at reading people, but precious few have been guides on the physical landscape. The conversation of the wilds includes landmarks. Landmarks in the wilderness are like street signs in the city. The best way to get in the habit of using them is to play the role of navigator even if with a person who knows the area. Pretend you are alone. Don't get hooked on the psychology of a passenger. Passengers only know that they got from one place to another, but don't recall how they got there.

When starting a trip, survey the land and try to picture where your destination lies even though you can't see it. Pull out the map and look for the most dramatic features you will encounter and the smaller features in between. Primary features might be cliffs, a pond, a river, a peak, or a river junction. Intermediate features might be side canyons, rock outcroppings, an aspen grove, or a knoll. For example, count how many side canyons there are between the starting point and the cliffs. Or estimate how far it is from the marsh you're skirting to the switchbacks on that 500-foot rise.

Counting stream crossings is not reliable. Often the route of the trail may have changed somewhat over the years. Even perennial streams may be dry when you get to them or may sink underground.

As you travel, always keep in mind where you are on your route—what you just passed, what lies ahead, and what lies behind. Take in the broad picture as well as the immediate. Check maps during breaks to make sure you're where you think you should be. Don't just put your nose to the grindstone and doggedly follow the trail. Trails have a tendency to disappear or multiply into a confusing labyrinth of game and side trails. If you pay enough attention to landmarks, you'll know approximately where the right trail should be. If the trail does meander off into nowhere or disappear on the edge of a meadow, return to the point where the trail was or where you knew exactly where you were. From there, as suggested by pioneer wilderness writer Bradford Angier, like the spokes on a wagon wheel, strike out in slightly different directions until you find the route again. Keep returning to home base until you've found the route. Should the trail disappear completely, you should be able to find the way to the planned campsite anyway by using a map, landmarks, and a compass. If, however, for any reason, you doubt your bearings or that you'll be able to find the way out, turn back or camp before getting lost.

Almost every woman surveyed had been lost at one time or another. Areas of little topographic relief, deep woods, numerous game trails, and intersecting and multiplying side canyons (such as the Canyonlands of the Southwest) are easy places to get lost. One woman, while lost in the woods, climbed a tree so she could see to locate landmarks. Another, while on a day hike, followed the smoke of a camp fire.

Following streams works if you know for sure that the stream you're following drains into the river you want to find. But in a remote wilderness, streams may lead only to places where they sink into the ground or end in a pond. Streams are also usually surrounded by willows, brush, and marshes and make very hard going. Keep to the high side of them where overland journeying is easier. Should the stream lead you to a lake or sink, you should be able to locate your position with a map and compass. If in an area of numerous lakes and ponds, use the one you found as a fix to determine where the other ones are. Eventually, working on the wagon wheel premise, you can figure out where you are.

Cross-country navigation is best learned slowly. The ideal way is to set up a base camp and make brief journeys away from it, slowly expanding your distance as you become better at navigating. Again, carry a map and compass. Stay within a carefully defined area such as a valley. Don't cross saddles (low points between drainages) or ridge lines unless absolutely certain of the way back.

Choosing a Campsite

Sometimes you don't have a choice of where to camp. Some areas are so overused that you must register ahead of time and camp in preselected areas. Know what is required before venturing into unfamiliar areas.

If you do have a choice, there are several items to consider: wind, water, fire, temperature, regulations, sleeping area, and solitude.

Your desire to use or avoid the wind, will partically determine where to locate your campsite. In an area where it may

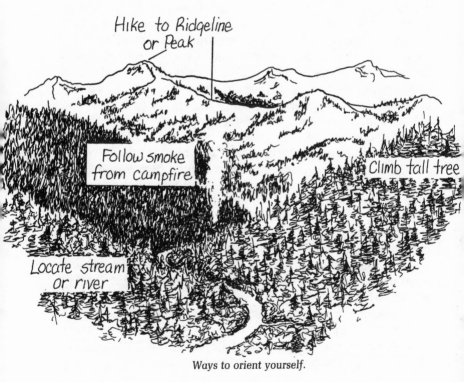

Ways to orient yourself.

become cold, wind will make it colder. Although the thermometer may register 20 degrees Fahrenheit, the windchill factor can make the temperature minus 20 degrees or colder, depending on the wind's speed. While the wind may not bring cold, it can become distressing if it is incessant. In areas heavily infested with mosquitoes or flies, the wind may be a relief. As flying insects prefer the doldrums, a steady breeze will make them seek less turbulent pastures. A breezy area is also pleasant in hot country. Near large lakes there is often a wind because of the water's cooling or heating effect on the surrounding air.

Behind or near a cluster of trees or rock outcrops, away from ridges, in bowls and sheltered valleys are the best spots for your tent when you want to avoid the wind. Exposed areas, without natural barriers, such as ridge tops and peaks, have the greatest amount of wind. These areas are usually unsuitable for camping because of their exposure, lack of water, uncomfortable terrain, and fragile ecosystem. However, they can be havens from heat or insects.

The tent opening should face perpendicular to a canyon so it is not exposed to up-canyon or down-canyon winds. Another good placement of the opening is facing protective tree or rock shelters.

In desert areas, camp in the shade. Don't camp too close to the water source or on game trails, since you may cut an animal off from its only water supply as in the following story.

Things That Go Bump in the Night

I'll never forget the first night I spent alone in the wilderness. I seriously doubt that I slept one bit. I heard every noise that was made and then some; I created monsters to accompany the noises.

Night is not a quiet time in the wilderness. Many creatures are finding food, exercising, and checking up on each other. They are not concerned about your sleep.

Some people like to listen to the sound of coyotes. If I have a rip-roaring fire and several companions for conservation, their calls are just part of the night symphony. But when I'm alone, I'd swear I've seen the whites of their eyes outside the circle of fire. Their howls bring to me an acute awareness of being alone that other night sounds don't bring.

There is one night that is more memorable than any other. It was dark and the stars were very bright. The moon had not yet risen. I was sleeping on a large, smooth rock next to a big water hole.

The water hole was one of the remaining few in the wilderness at this time of year. The rains had not come; last year was a drought; and the stream had almost completely disappeared. The temperature on the hot, sandy trail was 115 degrees, and the pool had kept me from heat exhaustion.

It was here I bedded down. Since it wasn't a "legal" campsite, I could not build a fire, so my meal was cold, which was all I wanted after a long, hot day anyway.

I was dreaming a beautiful dream when I heard a crashing sound. There was the spilling of rocks and splashing in the stream. It was much louder than the sounds I'd heard in the past of coyotes or deer, much like a person who'd just dislodged a wasp's nest.

I heard a snort above me.

I looked up. There stood a black bear, equally shocked, about three feet from my head.

We stared. And stared. And stared.

The bear seemed a huge-enormous-gigantuan to me . . . I was staring at him while lying on my back with my arms straight-jacketed in the sleeping bag. Not a comfortable situation, no indeed.

Hours passed.

"This can't do," I thought. "I must act."

Out came my arms. But what was I going to do with them? Strangle the bear?

I picked up my small, aluminum shovel (thank goodness it was next to my head) and banged it on a rock.

The bear snorted again. He began to walk away. We were still staring at each other. I was still lying in my prone position on the ground.

I thought, "This still won't do. He is only *walking* away. His departure is not fast enough."

The radio. The accursed ten-pound radio that didn't broadcast out to anyone the Forest Service made me carry . . . that would save me!

I pushed the squelch button. The echo of the squelch sounded like a gun going off in the canyon.

Crash, bang, swish. The bear took off. He was *running*.

The radio ploy had worked.

I went back to sleep. Suddenly, I felt something wet on my forehead. I didn't open my eyes. I just couldn't. "Oh, no," I thought hysterically, "the bear has come back and *his nose is on my forehead!*"

My eyes still squeezed shut, I slowly, very s-l-o-w-l-y, edged my hand up from my sleeping bag. Whapp! I slapped the wet spot.

It was a little tiny frog! I was in the path of a frog migration. For about an hour, I could feel the plip, plop, plop of the frogs on my face, hands, and sleeping bag as they hopped to the pool. The full moon had risen and they were on their way.

I fell asleep again. Suddenly I felt little wet things again on my face, and the familiar plop, plop. The moon had set and the frogs were migrating home. I found a few of them squashed under my sleeping bag the next morning.

If you got anything from this story, remember not to sleep next to watering holes—unless you are fond of bears and frogs.

In bear country, the campsite must be bearproofed. A Forest Service pamphlet titled "Backpacking" advises pitching the tent 125 feet upwind from the cooking area and the food and garbage. Put the tent exit near a climbable tree. Although black bears can climb trees, adult grizzlies cannot. Hang your food and garbage 10 feet above the ground, 5 to 10 feet from the tree trunk, and 3 to 6 feet below the limb on which it is hung so the black bear can't reach it. A clean campsite without alluring odors will help you get a good night's sleep without furry visitors. If a bear does investigate, it will go for the food rather than your tent or backpack. Never, never keep food in your tent.

Water is extremely valuable in the wilds. You can survive days without food, but can die within three days without water. In selecting a campsite, water should be nearby but far enough away that food scraps, fire remains, and human excrement will not pollute the water supply, including during snowmelt and floods.

Campsites should not be located on flood plains or other water drainages. They should be 200 feet from a lakeshore and at least 100 feet from a stream. In desert country, death by flash flood is a very real possibility. Camping on canyon bottoms should be avoided when possible and especially if there is a threat of rain. Look for watermarks on canyon walls that indicate how high previous floods have been.

Choose an area away from the trail. One woman reported laying out her sleeping bag on the comforting sand of the Snake River in Idaho's Hells Canyon. Since it was dark, she didn't notice anything unusual. Once the morning broke, she was awakened by a clang and clatter and the tromping of many hooves. As she rubbed the sleep from her eyes, she looked up

to see a string pack of horses ambling down upon her. She had put her sleeping bag right on the pack trail.

Besides avoiding four-legged creatures, camping away from the trail means privacy. For lone women, this seclusion is especially important. Since many people are in the backcountry specifically to be alone, it is considered polite to place your tent away from view.

After you've gone to the trouble of finding a level spot, you've got to clear away the debris. To narrow down the mishaps before setting up your tent and laying out your sleeping bag, go over the ground on your hands and knees and feel for bumps, roots, and dips. When preparing the sleeping area, plan to lie with your head facing uphill. If sandy soil is available, you can scoop out a contour for the hips. Since women have broader hips than men, they may want to dig a little contour for this part of the body, then lay the sleeping bag over it. The same can be applied for the shoulder area.

If camping without a tent, do not unroll your sleeping bag until you are ready to crawl in since it can become damp. Use a tarp and foam mattress under the bag both for comfort and to prevent the ground moisture from getting to you.

The old Boy Scout method of cutting green boughs, collecting moss, and in other ways drastically altering the campsite to create a comfortable sleeping area is no longer acceptable. Trenching to allow water to run away from your sleeping site is also becoming a thing of the past.

The Hearth

Should you or should you not build a fire if wood is available? If you do build one, where will it be safe?

Oftentimes, *who* shall build the fire is a point of debate when hiking with partners of the opposite sex. Most men will consider the fire building task their domain. Most women have forgotten the skill that has aided women as guardians of the hearth since the days of ancient Greece. Women were fire builders and keepers in the family unit until the advent of gas stoves. It is a wilderness skill that must be once again acquired because, like navigation, it is an essential. One of the women surveyed said being a Girl Scout had helped her because she "can build a fire anywhere." Fire building is also one of the distinct pleasures of camping.

Contrary to popular rumors, Smokey the Bear, at least the symbolic Smokey, is alive and well. The bear cub that was rescued from a forest fire and dubbed "Smokey" died some years ago, but the singed little animal is still a clarion to take all the usual precautions to ensure a safe fire.

Although there are times when a fire is good for regrowth of vegetation as a wildlife food supply, those times also require firefighters and all their equipment to keep the fire in check. Some land management agencies allow "natural burns" or fires

WESTERN PORCUPINE

Game trails are sidewalks for animals. If you sleep on or near one, expect some night traffic since many animals are nocturnal.

started by lighting or other natural causes to continue to burn. Although this practice is still controversial, it does go on. Before you enter a wilderness area, check the sky for indications of a natural burn or perhaps a wildfire. Again, you might check with the agency which manages the land as to the location of fires.

Don't build camp fires in high alpine country unless absolutely necessary for survival. These areas have a short growing season. The vegetation is delicate and one person can do a lot of damage. Trees are rare at high altitudes, and wood becomes increasingly scarce as you near and cross the timberline. If camping in these areas, definitely plan to use a stove.

Those going beyond developed campsites with ample wood supplies should also carry a portable stove. When the weather turns to snow or heavy rain and all the wood gets wet, you will have an alternate source of heat.

While a fire is romantic and part of the fun of the outdoors, there are many places where open fires are not allowed. Be sure you know the regulations before you start the trip. In some areas of the country such as Idaho, Utah, Montana, and Wyoming, where numbers are still small on the trails and wood is often plentiful, fires are still ethical and legal.

If open fires are allowed, choose a spot fairly close to your sleeping area, but away from the trees. Sparks from a fire can light up a tree limb or your tent, or sleeping bag. Consider how far a wind could snatch the sparks in the direction of your tent, tarp, and other gear. Heat and coals also can ignite a tree root and smolder for days. Don't build fires next to large, visible rocks. The fire will scar the rock and leave a permanent message to future visitors.

Build your fire on bare soil with debris cleared from around its perimeter to avoid starting a wildfire. Keep a quart of water on hand in case a spark escapes, and never leave the fire burning unattended.

In grassy or turf areas, dig up a layer of top soil or duff. This can be placed aside and kept cool and moist. When you are ready to leave, you can refit the pieces so no sign of the campfire will be left.

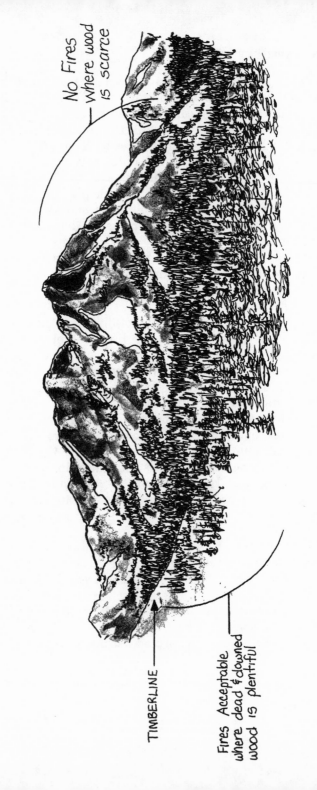

No Fires where wood is scarce

TIMBERLINE

Fires Acceptable where dead & downed wood is plentiful

Kitchen

There is some debate about using smaller rocks around the perimeter of the fire. Since fire blackens these rocks too, some oppose it and assert further that the rocks don't help keep the fire within the allotted space. If camping during fire season (usually midsummer), and in exceptionally dry areas, use rocks as a buffer. They do serve as a barrier for fire containment. In other areas and seasons, a good job of ground clearance around the area of the fire should suffice.

Whenever you come across an existing fire ring, use that instead of building another. There's no need to proliferate fire rings, as too many of them make the area look trashy. If the existing ring is in a bad location, destroy it and build another. Some areas have permanent fire pits built by a backcountry patrolperson. In these places, be sure your fire is dead before leaving. Scatter the ashes and leave the fire pit in the same condition or better than you found it.

Keep your fires small. Avoid "white man" fires where everyone has to sit far away from the fire because it is too big and hot. Build "Indian" fires which are small, use less wood, and are pleasant to sit around. The rule is to try to keep your wood thumb size. This type of dry wood is plentiful and lying about all over the ground in heavily wooded areas. One, large, dry piece of wood can provide a good backlog for the other wood to lie against and it also serves as a reflector of heat. After the backlog has burned it will be a fine source of hot charcoal.

Before starting the fire, gather enough wood for dinner and breakfast. For convenience and order, firewood can be sorted into three piles: small scraps for kindling; thumb-sized wood for most cooking and heat; and a few large pieces for after meal relaxing, night warmth, and light for reading and writing.

As a rule, the less compact a piece of wood, the better and quicker it will burn. If it feels fragile, it is a good source of tinder. If it is hard and heavy, it should be useful as a sustaining source of heat. If milky with sap, not only will it burn poorly, but the flame will spit and sputter.

Naturally, the wood should be dry. Green wood, preferably green boughs, can be used as a distress signal because it puts out a lot of smoke.

Some campfire enthusiasts love the smell of campfire smoke. Certain woods give off nice aromas. Others are very smokey, burn quickly, or have an unpleasant smell. Soft woods, such as pines, are good for starting fires and producing hot, intense, fire quickly; they also burn rapidly keeping you on your toes to keep enough in supply. Hard woods, such as cedar, are difficult to use for starting a fire and burn slowly. Driftwood, deposited beside streams and lakes, is a good firestarter if sufficiently dry. In semi-desert areas, dead mountain lilac and mountain mahogany are good fire material.

Standing dead trees should not be a source of firewood. These "snags" are the only homes of a variety of birds and other small creatures. Deadwood on the ground also serves a purpose to the land. As it decomposes, it becomes a vital part of the topsoil, provides nutrients, and a home for ants and other insects. If deadwood is scarce, let the remaining pieces nourish the land, and use your stove.

A quick scrutiny of your campsite will probably unveil masses of tiny twigs lying on the ground. These, along with dry grasses, leaves, and paper, will be the kindling for the fire. If the twigs don't break easily, they are not dry enough. During heavy precipitation, when the large wood is soaked, you can still crawl under a tree and find dry twigs and other dry wood. Collect enough kindling not only to start the fire but to reignite it should the flame falter. This usually requires about three large handfuls.

Wood that is best for a wilderness fire shouldn't require the services of an ax. To break wood, prop it against a rock and jump or step on it. An alternate if you aren't wearing heavy boots, is to hoist up a rock and drop it on the exposed limb. A third method is to hold the branch high over your head and smash it against a rock. All three methods pose the hazard of wood splintering in all directions, so close your eyes and avert your head and upper body upon impact.

There are three ingredients for a fire: oxygen (air), fuel, and heat. Although it seems obvious, oxygen is usually the ingredient the novice will overlook. Too much wood and too little air will suffocate the flame. Build the fire loose with plenty of air pockets between the ground and the kindling, and the kindling and the individual pieces of wood. As laying pieces of wood parallel to each other also chokes off the oxygen, crosshatching the wood works best. Sometimes blowing on a reluctant fire will get it going with more enthusiasm. Fanning the flame is another method.

Be sure the fire is dead when you leave a campsite. Dead means that you can touch the coals and rocks with your bare hands. To extinguish a fire when breaking camp, let it burn up all the charred wood, then pour on a lot of water. Stir the ashes about to make sure it is actually out. In hot summer months, wilderness areas are often a timber box. Should your fire escape and cause a wildfire, you can be held legally and financially responsible for the damage which can run into five figures.

When breaking camp, scatter all evidence of your fire. Place needles, leaves or duff over the bare spot. Be sure to carry away all your aluminum, tin foil and garbage that did not burn in the fire.

Litter and Other Insults

When women were asked what was the thing they liked least about a wilderness area, the most often cited complaint was litter. It's hard to tell how men react to this slovenliness, but revulsion toward it is universal and vigorous (3), and the man whose sink breeds ominous strains of bacteria is probably just as offended by litter in the backcountry as a woman. However, most of the articles written about the backcountry ethic and low-impact camping are authored by women.

Burying garbage is not feasible in the backcountry. Wild animals will dig it up and scatter it about. In popular areas, entire campgrounds become large middens. It takes years for the earth to degrade some natural garbage and centuries for some synthetics.

All food scraps should be burned, if possible, to avoid attracting wildlife to the campsite. If they cannot be burned, they should be carried out.

Three food scraps that are slow to degrade are orange peels, peanut shells, and egg shells. They are commonly found at campsites. Apple cores are popular with wild animals but in heavily used areas are seen by people before they are carried off by the wildlife. If you're in a remote area, apple cores and the like are not destructive, but too much of that sort of thing leads to a dependence of animals on people for food. It can lead to tragic results, as happened in Yellowstone National Park before open garbage pits were closed. The pits attracted the grizzlies, and the grizzlies attracted the people who came to watch them feed. The process culminated in the deaths of two young women and the deaths of the offending bears.

Most prepared backpack meals today are packaged in foil-lined containers. Hot water can be stirred directly in the container thereby reducing the need of dirtying another pot. The container can also serve as a dish. What to do with the foil afterwards? It can be burned, or at least most of it, if your fire burns hot and long enough. But this kind of fire, for reasons already stated, is impractical, unethical, and usually impossible. The most common solution is to burn the food scraps off the foil, then pick the remains out of the fire and stash them with the other trash in plastic bags. Washing the empty bags is acceptable if done away from water sources. However, this isn't advisable in bear country.

Don't wash dishes in lakes and streams with soap, including biodegradable brands which do not degrade instantly. Even though biodegradable brands eventually degrade, wildlife, fish, and the campers downstream won't appreciate your abuses.

Dirty dishes should be filled with water and scrubbed in a pan. One way to avoid using soap is to wash dirty dishes immediately with hot water, sand, dirt, and gravel.

When disposing of dishwater, garbage, excess noodles, corn kernels, and other delights should be burned or carried out. Small and large nocturnal visitors may be attracted to your dishwater so dispose of it far away from the campsite and stream.

In overused campgrounds you may, on occasion, encounter a legion of ants where food remains are in constant supply. Overly aggressive chipmunks, squirrels, rodents, jays, and skunks frequent such popular camping sites. If you hike in areas where there are shelters, such as in the Snoqualmie National Forest in Washington or the Blue Ridge Mountains in West

Virginia, there will usually be a family of mice or a fearsome rat or two awaiting your arrival—and your food. These creatures can gnaw through your pack with ease and are most bold at night. Solutions are to leave some food as a distraction (the easy way out which encourages them to remain); hang all your food outside the shelter and far from their nest (the best solution although very bothersome); or kill them (a gruesome, questionable, and often impossible task). Usually these creatures will not bother you, it's your food they want; however, many backpackers can recall the feel of a rodent scurrying over their sleeping bag. A dog will usually keep these creatures at bay but you will probably lose a lot of sleep from the racket of the chase and the whining that ensues.

Fortunately, nature is very efficient in disposing of human feces with its own bacterial agents if the remains are buried no deeper than eight inches in the soil. Hike far off the trail and at least one hundred feet from streams, lakes, and other water sources. Using the cat method, dig a shallow hole with a lightweight shovel or garden trowel. If you are unable to scratch the surface to bury the waste, at least place a rock, bark strip, or twigs and leaves over it to save other visitors an unpleasant surprise.

Urination should also be done far from water sources. Its acidity can affect plant growth but in general, it isn't much of a problem, except possibly aesthetically when cross-country skiing or snowshoeing popular areas.

Some backcountry areas have strategically placed latrines. Although they often smell and are in disrepair, use them when available. They were put there because too many people use the area to allow everyone to wander off in the bushes. These latrines are not for trash and garbage.

When urinating, make sure that your pants are not in the way; that you are not squatting in vegetation that may be poisonous, sticky, or sharp, and that you are facing downhill so your feet don't get wet. Inform others where you are going and why so you won't find yourself with a red face. If in a situation with no privacy, such as a flat area or rock climb, a poncho offers at least some semblance of privacy.

When traveling with a large group, dig a long, shallow trench for a latrine if you plan to stay for any lenth of time in one area. Leave a trowel by the trench so a little dirt can cover the area used. A bandanna can be tied to a branch near the latrine as a signal that it is occupied. Cover the trench when breaking camp and scatter twigs and leaves over the area to disguise it.

Since it takes an extremely hot fire to distroy tampons and sanitary napkins, you may have the distasteful job of carrying them out. Like toilet paper, they should not be buried because they never really decompose and the odor attracts some animals. In grizzly bear country, always burn them.

It doesn't hurt a stream or lake if you submerge your body in it and clean yourself with you hands. But again, soap should be ruled out. A better approach to personal cleanliness is a sponge bath in which you take all the precautions you did with doing the dishes.

Friends who get dirty together won't notice or care if the others don't maintain the same degree of personal hygiene that they would given indoor plumbing. As Becky Lankford, a teen-age mountaineer with a formidable list of ascents, says, "You're not up there to look pretty. You're up there to enjoy the wilderness and experience it with people who care about the real you under the dirt."

For similar reasons, a woman doesn't need to be especially concerned about washing her hair in the backcountry. She most definitely doesn't need to carry shampoo since the all-purpose biodegradable liquid camping soaps can be used instead.

There are convenient alternatives to keeping your hair clean. If your hair is long, braids and hair clips will keep it out of your face and free from tangles. If you wear your hair long and free, it will capture twigs and dirt quickly and will often tangle and pull in the backpack. Wearing a hat or bandanna hides the dirt until you arrive back home. If the dirt and sweat really bother you and a good nonpolluting area in which to wash your hair is not available, salt or commercially prepared dry shampoos will alleviate the problem. These can be sprinkled in, rubbed on the scalp to absorb and free the dirt, then brushed out. However, it's hard to get all of the application out of your hair, and those little granules may be more irritating than the dirt.

Brushing your teeth is another campsite consideration.

Toothpaste leaves telltale signs on vegetation for weeks and months. Baking soda and salt are good alternatives. If you like toothpaste and hate the others, dilute it with a lot of water before rinsing.

All of this takes time. But the person who loves the country she is in and who wants to help keep it pristine will save some energy for ethical camping.

Your First Hike Alone

Before your first solo hike, be sure you have passed all the other tests: you are confident of your hiking ability; you have the thirteen essentials; you can read a map and compass and can navigate if you lose the trail; you have experienced several strenuous (bad weather, tough elevation gain, rashes of insects) backcountry experiences; and you're taken some day trips alone through difficult terrain.

You are ready for the final assault. To make it easier, go to a familiar area when the days are the longest. Go in far enough so you could not get out easily when the shadows lengthen, but don't do so far that help seems thousands of miles away.

The worst moments will probably be at twilight and just as you're heading for bed. Be sure to have plenty of firewood gathered, if a fire is allowed, to scare the ghosts. You will see all kinds of fancied things just outside the ring of firelight. The fire will make you feel warm and protected. Animals fear and respect fire, so all those beasties out there will stay away.

Many animals are nocturnal, such as raccoons, martens, and badgers, and roam at night searching for food. Most of them will not harm you and will go out of their way to avoid you. However, they will be very interested in your food, and you should take precautions to protect it.

At night each sound stands out in bold relief. You can hear the pebbles knocked together as deer cross the streams; the hoot of the owl carries in the clear night air; the coyote howls to her family on the far hill who echo back her call as they travel near your camp. You might hear the sparks cackle as they leap from a dying log on the fire. The stream will undulate singing louder and softer and sometimes you can hear voices and noises in its constant gurgle. When the full moon rises you will want to hide your eyes under the sleeping bag because it is so bright.

Most people report that their first night was one of sleeping and waking constantly. You may think you never slept, that you laid awake all night—maybe you did. But wasn't it wonderful? You did it—alone!

Although most of the experts advise against entering the backcountry alone, most of them do it. Perhaps, to be honest, they feel the number of people who should go "where no man dared go before" should be kept to a minimum.

People don't spend their normal days alone. They deal with people constantly, if only on a formal basis of exchanging "good mornings." Imagine spending several days at home alone, without the human noise of the telephone, television, or radio, or human images such as books and magazines. Now add to this new sounds, physical challenges, a new setting, and you have backpacking alone. It is an adventure into yourself and into the world of nature. If you aren't ready now, fine. Maybe the thought of complete solitude repulses you. But someday you should try it.

5

Fail-Safe for the Better Half

Although Angie Dickensen has been holding her own for so long in "Policewoman" that she's survived the hoods and thugs into second generation reruns, the debate about whether or not she can take it still lingers.

Historically, woman's sexual anatomy was thought to be vulnerable to injury. When the ovum was discovered in 1827, woman's role in the scheme of human reproduction was expanded from incubator to procreator. But in her newly elevated status, she still dared not knock about for fear of upsetting her reproductive organs. No one seemed to worry over the male cells, but just how safe were they when suspended to the dubious care of an athletic supporter?

A woman's ovaries sit inside a big sac of fluid. The ova within the ovaries are further protected by the mass of cells of the follicle. Further protection is provided by the other tissue surrounding the female reproductive organs. In contrast, the sperm rest inside the testes, which hang well below the protective nest of the male's lower abdomen. "A man's scrotum is much more vulnerable than a woman's ovaries," comments Dr. John Marshall, director of sports medicine at the Manhattan Hospital for Special Surgery. A woman's breasts are also not easily damaged. "There's no evidence that trauma to the breasts is a precursor of cancer," he says. (1)

While her anatomy does not make her more vulnerable to injury than a man, there are a myriad of factors unique to a woman which she should be aware of when planning a backcountry trip. By identifying them, the implication is not that a woman ought to be more cautious than a man. There are plenty of problems more common in men, such as heart disease and hernias, which could affect their backcountry exploration. Identifying the problems and precautions unique to a woman is a means of taking her out of the category of honorary male in which outdoor writers assume that everybody is the same and overlook her entirely.

Leg Injuries

Before puberty girls and boys are very similar, with the girls holding a slight theoretical edge when it comes to physical performance because they mature faster. When the female hormonal flow begins the ligaments loosen in most girls making them more flexible. Witness the fine gymnastics' record of young girls right at the edge between childhood and adolescence. Some experts speculate that this loosening also makes the female more susceptible to joint injuries and dislocations.

The female hormonal flow also aids in the maintenance of strong bones. Once the flow subsides, and menopause occurs, older women may become more likely to suffer breaks and fractures due to the weakening of the bones.

It has been suggested that a woman's wider pelvis angles the legs in such a manner that more stress is put on the knees and ankles. In a collection of related injuries such as shinsplints, tendonitis, and bursitis, excessive foot pronation (duck footedness) is a culprit. Although this is still debated, woman's wider pelvis apparently doesn't result in a duck-footed gait and the accompanying leg injuries. What can cause this defect in foot posture is a shortened Achilles tendon, another reason not to wear high heels too often. (2)

In the early stages of her wilderness exploration, a woman may develop more injuries than a man simply due to a lack of acquired strength. In sports training this is called overload and results when too much stress is put on a muscle, tendon, or ligament. The chances of it happening are small unless you really overdo it. Injuries can be avoided with physical training and a gradual approach to more difficult ventures.

One sports physician says that in his experience about two-thirds of the cases of shinsplints are reported by women runners. He believes that women are more prone to developing acute shinsplints in the early stages of a running program and are more likely to seek medical attention when shinsplints occur. Other physicians say they haven't noticed such a difference. (3)

Since bursitis, tendonitis, and shinsplints may plague a person who begins or increases backcountry activities, their identification and treatment are important. Again, the best cure is prevention, but you should know what they are and know how to treat them. They can become chronic if not handled correctly.

Bursitis is the inflammation of the cavity of lubricating fluid between a tendon and bone. Tendonitis is the inflammation of the tendons, and shinsplints refers to a collection of injuries along the shinbone the most common of which is a fatigue tear. In general, these are usually ailments that beset the beginner as a result of overuse and are more likely to occur on downhill stretches in which the muscle is pulled to its extreme.

All three can be distinguished from sprains, dislocations, and fractures by a gradual onset of pain and stiffness. You probably won't notice that anything is wrong for a number of hours. The pain is not usually disabling and can be relieved with aspirin. Lightly use (but not overuse) the affected joint in its entire range of motion to prevent the problem from becoming chronic. (4) If you experience any of these problems, decrease your mileage and load, if possible, until fully recovered. This can be very frustrating, and many people will overlook the injury with no adverse effects. However, ask yourself if it's worth it.

Knees are especially vulnerable in both women and men.

Architecturally, they are weak because they support so much weight and the joint bones never come in full contact with each other. Traveling over difficult terrain for long periods puts extra stress on the knees. Pay attention to it, and pain you feel in your knees. If you seriously damage your knees and don't get proper treatment, the result can be lifelong.

About 80 percent of knee injuries occur of the weak side of the body. (5) Frequently, one leg will be shorter and/or one foot smaller than the other.

Pay particular attention to your knees when developing an exercise program. If one leg is noticeably weaker, special attention should be given to it in your exercise program. Do exercises with the weaker leg to bring it up to par with the other. In addition to exercising, wearing hiking boots with heavy metal shanks will help strengthen the legs. Another preventive measure is to place an inset or padding in the boot of the shorter leg or smaller foot.

Stretching exercises, done during rest stops and in camp, will help reduce the chance of leg injury. Should you seriously injure a knee while in the backcountry, it should be splinted (branches will do) to keep the leg straight and the knee joint immobile. It's best then to hobble out straight-legged or, if possible, with companions helping you keep the weight off the injury. Although many knee injuries are handled with less radical measures, such as wrapping to control swelling, it's best to assume the worst since you don't know if your injury is a bone fracture or torn ligament. It may be an injury that is aggravated by movement.

Menses

Most researchers agree that menstruation itself doesn't impair athletic performance. Typically cited is the fact that women have set world and Olympic records while menstruating. In one study of isometric strength, however, women who were not taking oral contraceptives did register differences in endurance during the menstrual cycle. (6) The longest endurance was midway through the preovulatory phase. The shortest was halfway through the luteal phase. While this study corresponds

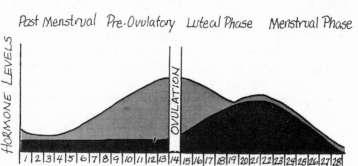

DAY OF CYCLE

with the generally weakened state some women feel prior to menstruation, the researchers found no difference in strength (as opposed to endurance) throughout the cycle. There was no difference in endurance in women taking birth control pills. In a study of maximal oxygen uptake, generally used as a barometer of physical fitness, there was no signficant change during the menstrual cycle. (7)

A few negative effects, besides cramps and inconvenience during menstruation, do occur directly before bleeding starts. They are caused by the levels of estrogen and progesterone in the body after ovulation. Water retention, which usually occurs three to five days before menstruation, may increase weight by several pounds. Women often feel bloated and uncomfortable, and experience backaches and a dull aching or heaviness in the abdomen. This happens because the hormones bind salt which retains excess fluid. Reducing salt intake at this time provides some relief. Whether or not premenstrual tension is the result of hormones has not been proven.

Menstruation itself is accompanied by a decrease in estrogen and progesterone levels, and water and weight loss. If she doesn't suffer from cramps, the woman may feel lighter and healthier. This hormonal change can also produce mild diarrhea. One woman said this was especially likely to happen if she was on a difficult hike and was having a difficult period.

Since it would eliminate seven days out of every month and the difficulties are usually minimal, it is not necessary for women to avoid strenuous activities during the luteal phase of their cycles. However, it is something to be advised of if you notice an otherwise unexplained decrease in performance.

Most women do not avoid wilderness activity during their periods, but many say it does interfere with or is affected by the experience. The most common complaint is inconvenience. Other complaints include greater than normal pain, pain that they experience normally which decreases their enjoyment, and earlier and heavier periods. One woman reported an apparent reduction of strength. Another avoids the wilderness as much as possible because, "I feel lousy, and am accident prone."

Many report irregularities, which include earlier and later onset, less cramping, either lighter or heavier bleeding, and shorter or longer duration. Kathryn A. Collins, a medical doctor and mountaineer, says that some increase in menstrual bleeding has been observed at greater altitudes.

What this all boils down to is that a woman should be prepared by always carrying sanitary protection. If prone to cramping, she should also always carry medication. Irregularity is common in the wilderness. It is not usually a cause for alarm and is probably related to the change in environment and circumstances.

Should menses come about when you are not prepared, bandannas and heavy socks are common substitutes. Socks filled with dry moss or grass are also suggested by some women. (8) If a baby is along, substitute a portion of a diaper.

A solution to the problem of disposing of tampons and Kotex in the backcountry is the use of sponges to absorb the menstrual blood. Natural sea sponges are marketed by several outlets. One such outlet is Sally Simmons Sponges, Box 189, Comptche, California 95427. Simmons recommends cutting the sponge to size. It can then be inserted, used, washed, and reinserted. The sea sponges can be boiled without shrinking or falling apart, unlike synthetic sponges, she says. Another source of such sponges is in an art supply store.

Some women miss their periods entirely while in the back-country. Stress or environmental changes can cause a temporary suspension of menses, called amenorrhea. "Recent studies show that stewardesses for international airlines are amenor-rheic because their biorhythms get all confused," says Dr. Penny Budoff, assitant professor of clinical family medicine at Stony Brook Medical School. Another physician comments that in life-or-death situations the pituitary gland will shut off the least important hormones, the gonadotropins [sex hormones.] (9) Amenorrhea happens to a lot of women involved in high-stress physical activities, comments Dr. Barbara Drinkwater, associate research physiologist for the Institute of Environmental Stress at the University of California at Santa Barbara. She says that it is an occurrence rather than a problem, and that overemphasis on it as a problem can be used to undo a lot of the progress that has been made in promoting women's sports.

Heavy activity or training does not, however, permanently impair the reproductive cycle. Once a woman ceases or de-creases the activity, normal menses will likely resume. (10) Amenorrhea or light menstruation is actually an advantage in the backcountry. A woman who experiences it should probably be grateful that the system is "on hold."

Painful periods, dysmenorrhea, can more accurately be called a problem. If you have never had menstrual cramps, the chances are that you won't experience them in the wilderness. Some male mountaineering and outdoor writers dismiss cramps by noting that, although they are common, most women have learned how to deal with them. Cramps, especially if they are debilitating, are a more serious problem in the backcountry than in the city where one can see a doctor or go to bed. Although many women experience lighter cramping that usual when hik-ing, climbing, and so forth, some feel the predictable and hurtful pangs no matter how accustomed they are to outdoor activity or how long they have been out in the field. It is frequently said that physically fit women experience less menstrual pain; while this may be true, it implies that a painful period is the person's own fault. Advice on this topic is mixed. Sometimes exercise will decrease the pain; other times rest is in order. Be your own judge.

One way to eliminate cramps altogether is to eliminate the period through birth control pills or minipills, but these create their own problems.

Contraception

When physical and mental stress is high, menstruation could be another irritant in an already difficult situation. In very cold, prolonged situations, disposal is a greater problem. Fuel would likely not be wasted to burn tampons and sanitary pads. Leaving them behind is unpardonable, since in cold temperatures the decay process (never complete even at higher temperatures and lower elevations) is next to nonexistent.

Some female wilderness users suggest taking birth control pills continuously for one or two cylces to prevent bleeding. "Since the pill and altitude both carry a small but definite risk of thrombophlebitis, the benefits of the pill should be carefully evaluated," said Dr. Kathryn A. Collins when she spoke at the Mountaineering Medicine Symposium 4 held in the spring of 1980 in Yosemite National Park.

If you choose to do this, the safest pills may be those that contain the least estrogen. Clotting abnormalities are known to be directly related to the presence of estrogen in birth control pills. However, the other component of the pill is progesterone. Careful studies to determine the degree of thromboembolic risk with progesterone have not been performed and cases have been reported in women using these products. (11) Most pills now marketed contain below fifty micrograms of estrogen and higher doses are not generally considered safe in any circumstances. Pills containing less than fifty micrograms of estrogen might be worth considering for wilderness use. Before using a minipill or low-dose pill, test it first as its use may result in minimal but prolonged bleeding.

Women should not begin a birth control pill regime just before entering the wilderness, since the side effects will be unknown. Many of the dangers of birth control pills are increased if a woman has hypertension, vascular problems, or diabetes. They are also increased by obesity, age, and heavy (fifteen cigarettes a day) smoking.

Among the less serious side effects are water retention, nausea, and weight gain. Water retention and weight gain have implications for the outdoorswoman because they can cause leg cramps. Other symptoms may include swelling of the face, hands, feet, and ankles, and other extremities. Although this can be uncomfortable, it is not considered particularly hazardous.

The more serious side effects of birth control pills, clotting and hemorrhaging, strokes, and heart attacks, can be dangerous because medical attention is not close by. High altitude mountaineering poses a small but increased risk of developing clots in the veins (thrombophlebitis) and lungs (pulmonary embolism). (12) Should a clot work itself loose and block the pulmonary arteries, it could be fatal. Factors which increase the risk of clotting are inadequate fluid intake, the increase in the number of red blood cells at high altitudes, stress, lack of oxygen at high altitudes, cold, heavy packing, immobility, and standing in one position for long periods. (13) Prolonged excursions at lower altitudes may also contain the risks or inadequate fluid intake, stress, cold, and heavy packs.

Since birth control pills add another risk to an already long list of predisposing factors, some people in the field of high altitude mountaineering physiology recommend that women discontinue their use at least one week before an expedition. (14)

Strokes are also a possible hazard since dehydration and an increase in the number of red blood cells (at altitude) may increase their likelihood. Although a heart attack is not directly aggravated by backcountry conditions, its occurrence in such conditions could be very serious since medical help would likely not be available.

Other adverse reactions associated with birth control pills which are of interest to a high altitude mountaineer are retinal thrombosis and optic neuritis. Field surveys conducted recently on trekkers in the Himalayas have shown a greater incidence of retinal hemorrhage in women than men. (15)

An intrauterine device (IUD) should not be inserted just prior to a trip to the backcountry. Since these devices can cause pain and cramping, increased and longer menstrual flow, spotting, backaches, and anemia, the user should make certain her body has adjusted to the device before venturing far from a doctor. Although perforation of the uterus and cervix, embedment, and other problems are rare, wilderness conditions would make such difficulties hard to deal with.

Infections and Other Maladies

An appendicitis is the most common ailment that requires evacuation from the backcountry. (16) It occurs most often between the ages of ten and thirty, and ranks high as a fatal disease of children between the ages of ten and fourteen. It is twice as common in boys as in girls.

Many infections and maladies of the female sex organs can mimic the symptoms of an appendicitis: acute salpingitis, gonorrhea, menstrual pain, middle pain, an ovarian cyst or tumor, or tubal (ectopic) pregnancy. Appendicitis is almost always cause for immediate evacuation from remote areas. With two exceptions, these others are not. The best way to separate female reproductive system maladies and others, such as a plain old sideache, from an appendicitis is to know the symptoms.

An appendicitis may be confused with these things because the appendix is located very near the right ovary and fallopian tube. If any of these problems occur on the right side of the abdomen, the distinction between them and an appendicitis is often difficult to make. Remember, it is possible to have any of these maladies and an appendicitis at the same time.

When the appendix becomes inflamed and infected, the infection can spread so rapidly that rupture may occur within a matter of hours. Rupture of an appendix can lead to peritonitis, the inflammation of the abdominal cavity. Because peritonitis is so serious, an appendicitis is best treated by immediate surgery.

An early symptom of appendicitis is pain in the mid abdomen. There are usually no cramps. Within a few hours the pain

will shift to the right side of the abdomen. Although consti-
pation may be suspected, do not take a laxative or enema since
the movement of the bowels can cause the appendix to rupture.
During midstages, there will often be vomiting, nausea, and a
low fever. As the infection develops, rebound pain as well as
referred pain will occur. Rebound pain is an immediate and
sharp pain that occurs when pressure exerted over the tender
area is suddenly released. Referred pain happens when pressure
in one area of the abdomen results in pain to another area and
is caused by the movement of the intestines as they shift away
from the site where the pressure is applied. Pain may abruptly
disappear when the appendix ruptures. It may also ease off
should the infection remain localized and form an abcess. In
the case of rupture, the pain will usually return but be more
diffuse as the infection spreads into the abdominal cavity. If
the pain remains local, or even if the symptoms appear to ease
off, the abcess may be merely biding its time to rupture at a
later date. In most cases there will be a persistent low fever.

If an appendicitis is suspected, evacuation should be immediate and by stretcher if beyond the early stages. If antibiotics
are available they should be taken at once. Determine the antibiotic dosage by contacting a doctor before venturing into the
backcountry.

Salpingitis, Latin for "infection of the tubes," usually develops gradually in both fallopian tubes, however, the pain is often
greater in one side than the other. If the right tube is involved,
acute salpingitis can be impossible to distinguish from an appendicitis. Symptoms which may occur in both are nausea and
vomiting, tenderness, muscle spasm, and rebound pain. A
symptom which should differentiate the two is pain or tenderness in both sides of the abdomen. A high fever indicates
acute salpingitis since it is generally absent in an appendicitis,
except in some cases when the appendix has ruptured. Salpingitis is usually a gonorrheal infection that has worked its way
into the fallopian tubes. Sexual contact followed by the symptoms of gonorrhea may indicate salpingitis. It generally takes
ten days or more for the infection to spread to the tubes.

Gonorrhea does not usually show early symptoms in women.
Symptoms can occur within five to seven days or longer after

exposure. Women may develop discomfort in the lower abdomen. There may be a period burning urination and vaginal
discharge. Often the symptoms are on again, off again, until a
full-blown infection emerges. A gonorrheal infection may initially be hard to differentiate from the onset of an appendicitis
since both may be accompanied by general abdominal pain.
However, in an appendicitis, the pain shifts within a few hours
to the right portion of the abdomen.

Gonorrhea is especially destructive in women. Often it is not
detected until it has spread throughout the reproductive system.
Treatment with penicillin or tetracycline should be immediate.
Untreated gonorrhea is women can have a number of serious
repercussions such as sterility, arthritis, and heart disease.

Menstrual pain may occasionally be confused with the vague
abdominal discomfort accompanying the onset of an appendicitis. However, cramps are usually absent in an appendicitis.
Since menstrual pain is very uncommon in women with no
history of it, abnormal abdominal pain can indicate an appendicitis. This is especially so if the pain becomes progressively
worse and becomes localized in the right portion of the abdomen.

Middle pain (mittelschmerz) occurs at the time of ovulation,
about midway between periods. Normally ovulation does not
cause pain, but slight cramping, and occasionally severe pain,
can occur. Although women who experience middle pain usually have had it before, in rare cases it can happen for the first
time to an unsuspecting female. Middle pain can be distingu-
sihed from an appendicitis if there is vaginal bleeding and the
symptoms occur midway between periods. Symptoms should
disappear within about one day.

There are many different kinds of ovarian cysts and tumors.
Some are serious, some are not. In general, pain resulting from
these is localized in the ovary and is not preceeded by abdominal discomfort. If you are prone to developing cysts, an exam
is in order before taking an extended wilderness trip. If a cyst
ruptures, there may be internal and abdominal bleeding. In
severe cases, there may be painful cramping and hemorrhaging.

Tubal pregnancies are insidious because they are often hard
to detect. A woman may have missed one or two periods, yet

a pregnancy test may show up negative. The presence of a tubal pregnancy is usually marked by recurrent and light bleeding. Should the pregnancy go undetected, the egg may burst through the narrow tube as it grows. When this happens, the woman may feel pelvic pressure and the need to urinate. This is usually followed by sudden and severe pain and a collapse.

In both ruptured cysts and ruptured tubal pregnancies, the woman may have excessive bleeding or hemorrhaging. Evacuation should be immediate. In the interim, packing the vagina with tampons, gauze, or sterile cloth may help slow the bleeding.

Urinary tract infections are fairly common in women because a woman's urethrea is so much shorter than a man's. The presence of the female hormones helps to ward off these infections, hence the greater susceptibility of young and menopausal females. These infections are treated with antibiotics, which you should have in your medical kit when taking long trips.

Urinary tract infections are usually known by painful urination, pressure on the bladder, and occasionally fever and backache.

Other infections, loosely gathered under the heading of vaginitis, are usually indicated by fetid vaginal discharge, painful intercourse, and itching. The use of antibiotics for urinary tract infections and vaginitis can upset the balance of microorganisms in the vagina. This upset can lead to a monilia (yeast) infection. About one-half of all vaginitis is yeast infection. Distinguished from the others by the discharge that is white and curdled, it is treated with anti-yeast suppositories and creams. Since antibiotics, birth control pills, IUDs, and stress can upset the organic balance of the vagina, it is wise to carry vaginal suppositories during long trips. Yogurt with an active culture is advocated by some women to treat mild yeast infections. The medical establishment does not go along with this because of the lack of studies. However, some women insist it works. Vaginal suppositories should be kept cool. Pack them where they will be least exposed to heat.

Women at Altitude

Vitamin C is popular with many women because research

indicates it helps reduce excessive menstrual bleeding and may be beneficial for women who have a tendency to miscarry. It is also said to reduce fatigue and help ward off colds. However, high vitamin C intake and high altitudes don't mix. (17) Persons tested showed lower resistance to altitudes, and a lower fatigue threshold and susceptibility to altitude sickness are possible.

There is evidence that women are more likely to develop peripheral edema at altitude than men. (18) In one study, 15 percent of the female trekkers measured near Mt. Everest had edema in more than one area (such as the hands, face, and feet).

Peripheral edema, is not particular cause for worry. However, its presence suggests much more serious complications such as pulmonary edema. In pulmonary edema the air sacs of the lungs fill with fluid and block off air. Among the symptoms are shortness of breath, raspy breathing, tightness in the chest, weakness, a feeling of suffocation while trying to sleep, and decreased mental performance.

Peripheral edema is a warning sign which women in partic-ular should look for as an indication of further complications if it appears in multiple areas, especially the face and eyes, rather than just in the hands and feet.

Apparently there is no relationship between the occurrence of peripheral edema at altitude and that associated with the menstrual cycle. (19) However, edema is associated with birth control pills and pregnancy.

Before anyone rushes to the conclusion that women are more likely than men to suffer from various symptoms of acute moun-tain sickness, it is important to point out that other studies done at similar altitudes showed that in other ways women adjust better. Although the latter studies involved fewer sub-jects, various control factors such as age and overall physical fitness were similar.

Pregnancy

It is fairly well agreed by those in the medical profession that a woman not only can but should continue customary exercise when she is pregnant, if there are no complications with the pregnancy.

Sensible exercise is good for the pregnant woman because it strengthens and tones the muscles she will use during delivery. Among other benefits are improved circulation—important for growth of the fetus—and fewer complications during pregnancy. In one study, 80 percent of the pregnant athletes measured had faster deliveries than nonathletes. "Figures were the same for both top and mediocre athletes, suggesting that overall conditioning rather than ability (or strength) is the determining factor," concluded Jill Kelly, Jane Leavy, and Ann Northrop in an article they researched for the Ms. magazine July 1978 issue. They also noted that mothers-to-be who are in good physical condition and gain between twenty-five to thirty pounds experience little lowerback pain and have faster postpartum recoveries.

A pregnant woman should give more thought to her wilderness activities, particularly as the fetus grows. Distances may need to be cut, along with the weight carried in the pack. Since her body is now taking care of two, she may find that she tires more easily.

Brisk walking is the most commonly recommended exercise during pregnancy. It is easily adapted to backcountry trails. Pregnancy is not the time to try bushwhacking, bagging peaks, or going above your accustomed altitude.

New ventures can be undertaken, but nothing beyond one's ability. "You should expect as much of yourself as you normally would, given your overall physical condition," says Molly O'Leary Hudson, a photographer and outdoor recreationist, who hiked when she was six months pregnant.

A pregnant woman should avoid long bouts in the heat, hike during the cooler hours and nap in the shade when the sun is at its zenith. Water retention is greater during pregnancy, and heat increases the chances of swelling and potential injury. Pregnant outdoorswomen are therefore more susceptible to soft-tissue injuries such as sprains and strains.

It is important to insure adequate dietary and water intake.

Fluids should be replaced every few miles. This usually means drinking more water than you are thirsty for.

Things that can slow you down during pregnancy, such as morning sickness, resting during the middle of the day, and taking your time in general, are all reasons to be especially aware of whom you pick for outing companions. You'll want empathetic partners who won't grumble if you haven't broken camp by six A.M., or if you have to hoist off the pack and go behind a bush every half hour to urinate.

"The most important thing is to listen to your body. Let it guide you, then shift gears into comfortable and just go," says Dr. Charles Greenhouse, who has treated over seventy-five pregnant runners in his private practice in Silver Springs, Maryland. "If the exercise becomes uncomfortable, slow down." (20)

Dr. Greenhouse suggests not to exercise beyond the point of exceeding 65 percent of your maximum heart rate. This is to insure that the fetus is not deprived of oxygen. Although the impact of altitude on pregnancy is still controversial, excursions in thin air are not recommended because of the potential of decreased oxygen uptake affecting the fetus. Some studies show increased infant mortality and decreased birth weight when women not accustomed to high altitudes conceive and give birth at above approximately 10,000 feet. (21)

As mentioned before, the uterus is one of the best protected areas in the body. "In the early part of pregnancy, the fetus is well protected by the bones and muscles of a woman's pelvis," says Dr. Mona M. Shangold, an associate professor of obstetrics and gynecology at the Albert Einstein College of Medicine, Bronx, New York. (22) After the first trimester, the fetus is protected by the water bag. "The fetus seems to handle starts and stops and bouncing around quite well," she says. Generally, it is not until the end of the first trimester that the uterus begins to protrude from the pelvis. Even then, Dr. Shangold says, a woman with an uncomplicated pregnancy, and no history of spontaneous abortion or stillbirth, can probably handle some bumps without danger to the fetus.

During the first trimester, most mothers only gain about three pounds. Noticeable changes in performance generally show up after the first three months. But it is during the first trimester that the danger of abortion is greatest. Between 10 to 15 percent of all pregnancies end in spontaneous abortion. The majority occur during the second or third month while a few carry though to the seventh month. Because of the danger of spontaneous abortion, a pregnant woman would be well advised not to travel too far beyond medical facilities.

Morning sickness is another drawback. "I felt very sick at first," says Melissa B. Holsten, who worked as a field soil scientist up until her sixth month. "During the middle months I felt normal. Later on I tired much more easily."

During the second trimester, the obvious physical changes start to show. The uterus expands about twenty times and the woman gains about ten pounds. While the body adjusts to the shift in balance, the increased weight up front may make certain feats, such as balancing across logs over swollen rivers, more difficult. "I found a walking stick very helpful," says Cynthia Marquette, associate director of the Fairbanks Environmental Center, who continued her outings through the eighth month. She also comments that she was more easily tired than normal.

You may be accustomed to sleeping on the ground directly or with a foam pad. While air mattresses are more expensive and weigh more, the investment might be worth it as pregnancy makes it more difficult to find a comfortable sleeping position.

By your third trimester, the effects of pregnancy are at their greatest. Ligaments, which are already looser in women, will have loosened more. Because of this, knee and pelvic ligaments (along with the others) may be more susceptible to stretching and tearing.

In one study, women measured at thirty and thirty-eight weeks into pregnancy, and at three to six weeks after delivery, experienced a significant increase in knee ligament extensibility. The major increase (30.73 percent) was between thirty-eight gestation and three weeks postpartum. (23)

Because of the extra weight, impaired balance, and loosening of the ligaments, you are more likely to take a fall. Activities in which there is high risk of falling should be ruled out during the last trimester. They should also be approached with caution during the first and second trimesters. These might include alpine skiing, technical climbing, bouldering, glissading, and horseback riding. Should you be injured, sprains and strains can take longer to heal in the last trimester due to water retention and swelling. If injuries are not treated properly, they can become chronic.

Many pregnancies contribute to the development of varicose veins. This is due to the pressure of the fetus, which cuts off some of the circulation. If injured, varicose veins are more susceptible to phlebitis (inflammation) and hemorrhaging. An injury requiring bed rest during pregnancy also poses the risk of developing phlebitis.

Varicose veins contribute to fatigue in the legs, and if you have them, are yet another thing which can slow you down. However, hiking helps maintain muscle tone providing the veins with external support. In addition, the exercise helps get the blood moving toward the heart through the gnarled contours of the damaged vein.

Long periods of standing, in which the blood pools in the legs, contribute to the development of varicose veins. While on the trail, and off, lightweight support stockings counteract the pressure of the blood in the vein. When driving to the trailhead, take frequent stops to avoid sitting in one position too long. When sitting, elevate your legs or change their position. Tight garments, a minus in the backcountry anyway, increase the restriction of blood movement. Elevate your legs at least twice a day for thirty minutes. This applies even if you don't have varicose veins, as all of these suggestions will help prevent them.

Take extra care of your feet. Sweating and dirt, common to the outdoorswoman, can create an environment in your boot that can lead to skin infections. Infections may take longer to heal during pregnancy. Pay particular attention to changing socks frequently and keeping them clean.

Many of the chemicals that wilderness users ingest, including iodine for water purification, antibiotics, and others, should not be taken by a pregnant woman because of possible damage to the fetus. Before taking any drugs or chemicals during pregnancy, check with your pharmacist or doctor.

Premature labor can occur spontaneously or be induced by

a fall or severe blow. The backcountry is not the ideal place to give birth, nor is a premature baby likely to survive without hospital care. The closer you come to your due date, the closer you should stick to home.

6

Perils and Precautions

CITY DWELLERS LEARN not to run in front of trucks, grab onto power lines, drink household chemicals, or dangle out of fifth-story windows. They learn which areas and people to avoid. They don't give a great deal of thought to these familiar perils because they are familiar with them.

Because, for most people, the wilderness is not a customary environment, they must give extra thought to their actions. Unless a person is very experienced, survival techniques will not be second nature. They require thought, planning, study, and caution. They requiring learning how to cross a river without drowning, where to go during an electrical storm, what kind of conditions are likely to produce an avalanche, what to do if stranded in a snowstorm or if becoming lost, and what kinds of animals and plants are potentially dangerous.

Even if you are experienced, you are not immortal, nor are you incapable of making mistakes. Overconfidence is a killer. Learn what the risks are, and what to do about them.

148

In little-traveled areas, you are truly on your own, since the chances of a search and rescue mission finding you before it is too late are small.

If you do embark on a trip alone in an area in which you are not likely to encounter other people within a few hours, always let someone know where you are going. If you do not want to commit yourself to one particular plan, at least let this person know the exact names of the topographic maps of the area in which you will travel. Also, list the areas within these which you are most likely to visit. Do not go outside of the area included in your plan. This way, if you are late, your friends will know where to look. Otherwise, you can set off a sequence of events that will culminate in bringing in the National Guard. Bringing in the National Guard isn't easy. By the time someone convinces the authorities that you are worth looking for, it may well be too late. There is not a well organized force out there somewhere waiting to look for lost hikers. At best, such as in National Parks, experienced search and rescue teams take at least twenty-four hours to organize. At worst, they do not exist and must be assembled through county authorities, jeep clubs, mountaineering organizations, and your friends and family.

In most circumstances, your family must bear the high cost of hiring airplanes and helicopters in an attempt to locate you or your body. You, your campsite, or your car are usually difficult to spot from the air, so this could require a great deal of air time.

If you are out in field a great deal, carry radio equipment with you or at least in your car. A $150 investment in radio equipment can save you much money later.

Weather

Bad weather is the numero uno hazard. Once you enter the wilds, your jolly television weatherman, with his toothy smile, and repartee of kitsch and comic-book wisdom will no longer be with you. Your ability to read the weather will have to be better than his ability to boost television ratings.

Weather reading begins with a general knowledge of the types of weather common to a locale. If you make trips primarily in familiar areas, you still have to watch weather forecasts. If traveling to an unknown area, don't just leave it to fate and assume the weather will be what you are accustomed to. Rain chaps in wet coastal areas are a necessity, while in the Rockies most people have never heard of them.

The farther out of your area the trip will be, the earlier you should start planning. You may travel across the country to visit a mountain area only to find it's snowed in even though it's July. You may plan a trip in the Boundary Waters Canoe Area in Minnesota and be driven out by a perpetual drizzle.

Within the United States, there are three climate zones, and within these are east to west and topographical variations—and these are just generalities.

The three climatic zones of the United States, including most of Alaska, are warm (Southern California, Georgia), short winter (most of the continental United States), and long winter (Alaska). Within these zones, the wettest month of the year varies a great deal. Outings should be planned to avoid the wet spells. For example, in the Rockies, the plains, and Texas, these wet months are in the spring. In California, they are in the winter. The eastern parts of the United States have a more uniform annual distribution of precipitation.

Areas near large bodies of water, such as the oceans and the Great Lakes, vary less in daily and seasonal temperature changes than do the mountains and the dry plains and deserts. Take this into consideration when packing.

Clouds, and the weather fronts they accompany, are good indicators of what the weather is going to be like, especially if you know something of the other changes attending a front. The study of clouds and what they portend is something that most can pick up rather easily. Often, in the isolation of the wilderness, people are much more likely to notice a slight change than they would in ordinary circumstances.

A warm front usually means a long, dull bout of precipitation. In advance, the wind and humidity will increase while the temperature remains steady. The sky becomes gradually overcast with a cloud sequence of altostratus and nimbostratus. Visibility will be good at first, then slowly deteriorate. As the front moves in, the wind direction will veer, the temperature will rise slightly, and a low cover of nimbostratus clouds will settle in. Fog, mist, drizzle, and rain will gather tentatively and then with increasing authority.

The duration of a warm front can be interminable. In a warm front, you're faced with the decision of putting up with it or getting out. If you decide to wait it out, you may be waiting for days.

A cold front brings violent, brief changes. In advance, the

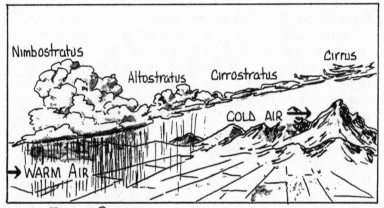

WARM FRONT PROFILE

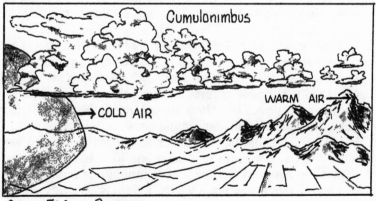

COLD FRONT PROFILE

wind will be steady, then more squally. The temperature will either remain steady or fall slightly. The humidity will not increase. The cold front is clearly marked by a bank of puffy cumulonimbus clouds. Distant thunder and lightning may occur. As the cold front overtakes you, there will be a marked change in wind direction and intensity. This will be preceeded by lightning, then accompanied by heavy rain or hail. As the storm passes, the clouds will usually break and lift. Rain will ease off within an hour or so of passage. Then there might be scattered showers with the sun breaking through at intervals.

The best thing to do in a cold front is simply to hole up. In the midwest, they are often accompanied by tornadoes.

Because of the altitude, the mountains have more extreme changes in weather than do the surrounding lowlands. These may differ not only with the change in altitude, but according to the side of the mountain. In addition, the temperature decreases about 3 degrees for every 1,000 feet of elevation gained in the mountains. Weather can change dramatically within hours.

Given a trip of more than a few days, storms in the mountains are a certainty. The closer to the summit, the worse the weather. If the couds, precipitation, and cold of the summit are not to your liking, usually the remedy consists of descending into a valley where you can watch the storms gather and assault the peaks while the sun shines warmly below.

Thunderstorms are of grave importance in the mountains, plains, desert, and on water. They are usually a midsummer phenomenon. If caught in one, stay away from ridges, peaks, towering or isolated trees, and any other feature that stands out on the skyline and attracts lightning as a conductor. If possible, get off the water or to lower ground. Find a spot far enough away from prominent features to prevent becoming part of the conduction process, but close enough not to become a target yourself. Find safer shelter among dense, small trees, or in a cave. If this isn't possible, huddle close to the ground and divest yourself of metal such as tent poles and pack frames.

The time between the flash of lightning and sound of the thunder tells you how far away the lightning is. Every second that elapses between the flash and the thunder puts the elec-

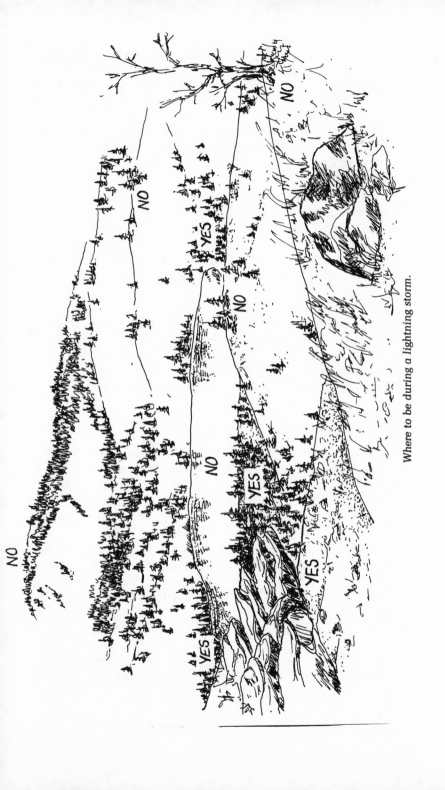

Where to be during a lightning storm.

trical charge about 1,000 feet away. If you only count a few seconds and you're on a ridge top, it's time to start moving, fast.

Thunderstorms in the canyon lands of the United States desert are equally serious. Flash floods are common and the risk of drowning or injury should be enough to give you pause. Thunderstorms can accumulate out of nowhere. Slim Woodruff relates the time she was hiking the Escalante River in Utah. It was raining and the men of the party wanted to camp in an overhang right next to the river. She talked them up to a cave high above the stream. "That night it did flood, and we would have been soaked down lower. We also discovered an unexcavated Indian ruin, so no one minded the extra climb," she says.

Fall and spring camping can be a real joy since the sun, insects, and people aren't as intense. But don't expect to get by with a picnic basket and an army blanket. It can get well below freezing, particularly if the night sky is clear with no cloud cover to insulate the earth. You could also encounter a snowstorm which can sock you in for several days—or more.

Crossing Streams

The sandy route through a stream may appear the safest, and the shortest point across may seem easiest. This is all well and good if you don't sink in the sand, and if the shortest route isn't used by every pack string that comes along. The route may have been worn away to an underground trail by the horses, as you'll soon discover when the water reaches your belly.

Bare feet are for dangling off the side of a dock or for splashing around in swimming pools; they aren't for wading unknown rivers. In swift streams, it's worth getting your boots wet in order to wear them as an anchor and for protection from the rocks.

Wade downstream at a diagonal with the current. Move slowly, keeping your legs spread at shoulder width for solidity and balance. A strong walking stick is helpful as a probe and an aid in balance. Hold the stick on your upstream side. Try it once and you'll know why.

A backpack can be an enemy if you take a fall in a river; the weight can hold you under while you struggle to unfasten yourself. Undo your waist belt before venturing across. The danger is especially great if you are crossing on trees or rock hopping from considerable heights. Find a way to get your pack across other than strapped to your back. A hint about slippery crossing: scatter the route with a little sand for traction.

If you have a good arm, you can lighten the load by pitching your sleeping bag, tent, and boots to the other side. Groups at stream crossings can form a pack brigade, in which each person stations herself in a secure position in the stream and passes the packs from one to another across the water.

River crossings that require the aid of a rope are good reasons to plan a different route. Using ropes is very time consuming and can be dangerous. Unless someone in your party is a Will Rogers, lassoing rocks or tree stumps on the other side of the river is unlikely. A careful swim or walk is the only way to get the rope across. Be sure the rope is long enough to allow for a diagonal journey across stream. Sometimes the rope can be secured on tree limbs and you can cross hand-over-hand like a Swiss tramway. Should you be forced to perform this maneuver, you'll greatly appreciate those many hours spent lifting weights to develop upper body strength.

Storms and spring runoff can swell streams and rivers beyond recognition. A minor wade in September can turn into a major ford when rivers and creeks are at flood. The greater the snowfall the preceding winter and the more rapid the thaw, the greater the volume of water. Cindy Shott, office manager for Yellowstone Wilderness Guides, says her most miserable experience was crossing waist-deep water while carrying a fifty-pound pack in a river fed by snowmelt. "Cold," she says, "with exclamation points!"

Snowmelt can raise water levels during a mere day hike or when you return to a river after several days. In the interim, the sun has been beating and the snow melting steadily. The creek may have risen to where you'll have to get serious and put on your wading shoes.

In California, a group of teenagers and their leaders were warned by a ranger against wilderness travel because of rains and swollen rivers. The group made it sixteen miles to a ranger shelter while it continued to rain. They were evacuated in a week later by helicopter. The rains had created monstrous rivers. Some members of the group said that the cracking of boulders smashing against each other in the maddened rivers kept them awake at night and made further travel impossible.

Kathryn Bulinski, a lands specialist for the United States Bureau of Land Management, recounts a kayaking trip on the Russian River in Northern California. Running a river at flood is much different than running it during normal conditions. Through a pouring rain they paddled. The harder it rained, the more miserable it became. She was afraid to pull into the bank because it was slumping; massive pieces of earth slid into the river, trees and all. She couldn't see well because the rain fogged both sides of her glasses. Her companion's boat capsized. All their gear got wet, which forced them to pull in and make camp. Then the tent didn't hold up in the downpour.

People have lost their lives to swollen rivers. Check out weather conditions before you set out on a trip. Running a river at flood is best left to experts and professionals.

Avalanches

Snow avalanches are in the same category as horrendous weather; they are killers. They are a year-round peril, although they are most dangerous in winter and spring. Thousands of avalanches track and thunder their way down the mountains every year.

Snow avalanches are a complex phenomena, not completely understood even by experts. They are impossible to accurately predict.

The loose snow variety of avalanche starts at a small point and rapidly increases in size and quantity as it moves downhill in a formless mass.

Most accidents are caused by a slab avalanche, which occurs when unstable snow breaks away from stable snow at well-defined fracture lines. Most victims trigger the slides themselves. Their weight on the snow slab breaks the fragile threads that hold it to the slope. Loud shouts, thumps, and noises may trigger a slide.

Molly O'Leary Hudson, who lost her husband to an avalanche, researched the subject afterwards. She advises to check for several danger signs: steepness, profile, aspect, and ground cover of the terrain. On a 30 degree (60 percent) or less slope, the chance of an avalanche is rare. Above this, it is much greater. Ground covered with trees, rocks, or heavy brush usually anchors the snow and thereby dissipates the onslaught. One inch or more of new snow, or layers of old snow subjected to melting—especially in large, exposed, open areas—are very dangerous. Convex slopes are more dangerous than concave, Molly says. During midwinter, north-facing slopes pose the greatest threat of avalanching, while south-facing slopes become hazardous in the spring and on sunny days when melting makes the snowpack unstable. Although slopes that protect you from the wind are more pleasant, they are more likely to slide since snow accumulates there in greater depth and is less compact than that on the windward side.

Avoid avalanche chutes (vertical passages where large masses of snow slide down the mountain) and cornices (piled snow that hangs over the edge of a mountain ridge or cliff). The safest routes are ridges (without cornices) and slightly to the windward side. (1) If you cannot travel the ridge, the next safest route is out in the valley, far from the bottom of the slope. If traveling a suspicious area, the best times to cross are early morning or late evening when the sun is not beaming and cooler temperatures help seal the ice crystals together.

If an area looks suspicious, and there is no safe alternate route, cross the snow one person at a time. Loosen pack straps. Free your hands from ice ax and ski pole straps. Loosen the bindings on skis and showshoes. Secure all your clothing; zip up your jacket, pull down your hat.

If caught in an avalanche, discard your equipment and try to swim to keep your head and body on the surface. If possible, try to swim to the edge of the avalanche. As you feel the movement slowing, get your hands in front of your face to make an air pocket for breathing. Once the slide stops, it hardens like cement. Survivors report that they can't tell which way is up.

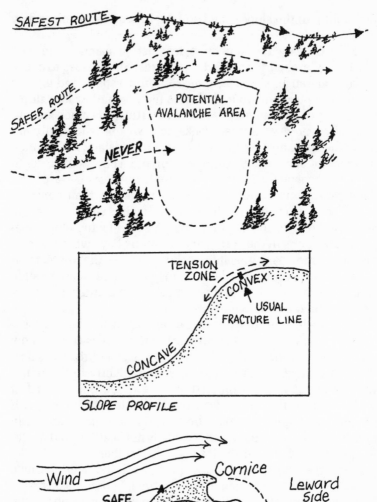

SAFEST ROUTE

SAFER ROUTE

POTENTIAL AVALANCHE AREA

NEVER

TENSION ZONE

CONVEX

USUAL FRACTURE LINE

CONCAVE

SLOPE PROFILE

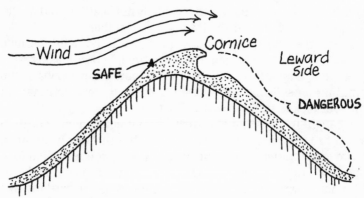

Wind

SAFE

Cornice

Leward Side

DANGEROUS

Shouting will do you no good. The victim can hear the rescuers but the rescuers can't hear the victim. Panic and screaming will just consume limited air.

Survivors should mark where the victim was last seen, then go directly downslope and immediately begin probing with a ski pole, stick, or ice ax handle. If time and the number in the party allow, send someone for help, as the more searchers, the better the chance of discovery. After one hour, the buried victim has only a 50 percent chance of living. A rescued person must be treated immediately for suffocation, shock, and hypothermia.

Linda Burke, who has been employed as a crew leader for the Youth Conservation Corps and has engaged in much winter recreation, says that the only time she feared dying was during a winter ski expedition in Idaho's Salmon River Mountains. "We were exposed to extreme avalanche danger for days. We could hear them and often crossed the rubble which marked their passage." Linda's crossing was made through precipitous mountain terrain. Perhaps, like many, she was aware the danger, but rarely is the reality brought home until you actually face it. She did not, however, indicate that she was sorry she had made the trip.

Rock avalanches are more often an annoyance than a death trap. Sometimes a domino effect occurs when a climber knocks a rock loose, which sets off others. If climbing in loose rock, stay clear of those above you until they are anchored in one position. Always be alert in rocky areas to the activities of others and if you dislodge a rock, shout "Rock."

One year several firefighters were killed in a rock avalanche. Because of their concentration on fighting the fire, the crew was unaware of two bulldozers on the ridge line, which were clearing a path to stop the fire's advance. The bulldozers dislodged several large boulders which resulted in a rock avalanche.

If your route crosses shale or small, loose rock, you will notice that the rocks slide downhill under your feet. If you stop, your weight may carry you downhill with the rocks. If the slope is steep, you may have to run to get to the other side.

If an agency in charge of a wilderness has posted an area as unsafe due to rock or snow avalanche, plan an alternate route.

Fire

If you notice a consistent column of smoke, sky darkening, ash trickling out of the sky, and the heavy smell of smoke, suspect a large fire. Climb the nearest ridge to determine how far the fire is from your location. If the weather is dry and hot, winds strong, and the fuels plentiful, look for a shortcut to the nearest road and safety because the fire can easily sweep toward your direction. Constantly check the fire's progress as you leave the area to be sure you are not walking into a fire trap. Fire can change direction quickly.

The best place to be when you are near a large fire is in the areas that have already burned. Fire burns best on steep slopes and in dry fuels, so head for rocky, bare soils devoid of vegetation. Wear cotton clothing layers all over the body, including a damp bandanna over the face. You cannot outrun a fire. If it's a small fire coming at you, you can run through the wall of flames (if wearing protective clothing) into the previously burned area. Immediately rolling on the ground will extinguish any clothing that ignited during your dash. Clothing doused in water is doubly protected.

Streams will not save you if you are caught in an intense fire. Fire depletes oxygen. You can die of suffocation, smoke inhalation, or seared lungs without a bit of flame touching your body. The best action is to leave the area ahead of time.

Raintree County

Hiking in swamps can be dangerous and exhausting. Swamps are usually flat with few landmarks. The soft soil and water suck at your feet in a constant drag. Sometimes the earth looks solid, but when you step on it, you sink up to your knees, waist, or even your eyebrows.

Quicksand won't suck you under like a hydraulic pump, but you'll go deeper as you struggle. Travel quickly over wet, standing sand. If caught, get your pack off quickly and try to semifloat and swim back to solid ground. Otherwise, keep still if you can't reach something stable and wait for help.

Beach Hiking

The two major hazards of the beach are getting caught in tides and not being able to locate drinkable water.

Know the tides. Look for high water marks so you won't be swimming in your tent before the night is through. You can get stranded on a beach bench or rock ledge while exploring. Should you feel the urge for a quick swim, know the tides. They can converge and pull you out very quickly. Ocean swimming requires both skill and strength, unless you find a quiet lagoon.

The fragile worlds of the sand dune and tide pool are great fun to explore, but easy to disrupt. They also have their dangers. Jelly fish, especially the Portugese Man-of-War, can give you a memborable jolt and horrendous welt. *Jaws* wasn't pure fiction. Sharks are worth thinking about before taking chances.

"Water, water, everywhere, nor any drop to drink," moaned the sailor in the *Rhyme of the Ancient Mariner*. Lack of potable water is probably the biggest deterrent to adventurous beachcombers. Saltwater is worthless because the salt content is so high that it will tax your existing body fluid.

Sun Exposure

Sunburning and tanning, even if there is a cloud cover, are hazards for the fair-skinned. Exposure hastens the aging process and contributes to keratoses (elevated, scaling, pigmented areas) and to skin cancer. After years of exposure to ultraviolet radiation, mostly in high altitude glacier country, one prominent mountaineer is now under treatment for basal cell removal. "Tell them to protect their skin," she said. Use a sunblock not a sunscreen.

Dark-skinned persons are less susceptible to skin damage from the sun, but all people must protect their eyes from snow blindness. Ultraviolet light can injure the cornea of the eye, particularly at high altitudes where there is less atmosphere to absorb the radiation. There is usually a delay in the onset of symptoms, which are pain and visual impairment. Usually the damage is not permanent, but sensitivity to light may persist for some time.

Altitude Sickness

Altitude sickness, or acute mountain sickness, is not a disease, but a problem caused by a decrease of oxygen in the air. Common symptoms are severe headache (a sign of cerebral edema), raspy or labored breathing, coughing, staggering gait, loss of appetite, nausea, and vomiting. Drowsiness is common, as are impaired reasoning and memory.

Prevention means gaining elevation slowly. Although altitude sickness can occur at 8,000 feet, it is more common above 9,000 feet. Do not ascend more than 1,000 feet per day at these elevations.

There is debate over the value of using acetazolamide as a preventative for acute mountain sickness. (2) This is a diuretic which may be beneficial in reducing the water retention associated with pulmonary edema. But, pro and con, researchers agree that the best prophylactic is acclimatization.

Those who become ill should avoid heavy work, breath deeply, drink extra liquids, and eat a light, high carbohydrate diet. Light activity is preferable to complete rest, as sleep only retards respiration and aggravates symptoms. Sedatives should not be used for the same reason. If the symptoms persist, seek lower elevations immediately. Continued exposure can make the victim too weak to travel. Those who experience mild altitude sickness, may be able to continue their climb after regaining their strength at a lower elevation.

One woman and her family climbed Mt. Rainer, the glacier-covered volcano of Washington and the second highest mountain in the continental United States. Two members of the family had altitude sickness. Her father was vomiting, and she could hardly breathe. She found that, although she was in excellent physical condition, she was so exhausted from trying to breathe that her legs wouldn't move. It took extreme willpower to force her legs to stagger the last 1,000 feet to the summit.

Hypothermia

Arctic explorers like Robert Peary, who lost eight toes to

frostbite while trying to find the North Pole, are not the only ones who have to worry about the cold. Hypothermia is a killer of outdoors persons. Hypothermia means a drop in the body's core temperature. One of the reasons it is so deadly is that the symptoms include dulled thinking and disorientation.

Getting cold and wet, being exposed to the wind, heavy exercise, and not ingesting sufficient fluids can all combine to cause hypothermia. A dunk in a cold river will get you started.

Besides knowing its causes, the best way to prevent hypothermia is to take action quickly once symptoms appear. Even a one-day trip requires caution. In bad weather, hypothermia becomes apparent within five to six hours. In severe weather, symptoms can come in one or two hours. The time between early symptoms and collapse in severe circumstances can be as little as one hour. The time from collapse to death can be only two hours.(3)

Several years ago, three women enrolled in a survival school were put on their own for two days and one night. Caught in an unexpected storm, they began to show signs of hypothermia: cold skin, numbness, shivering, slurred speech, drowsiness, difficulty moving their hands, stumbling, and forgetfulness. As the illness progressed, amnesia, weakness, a decrease in shivering, hallucinations, and apathy set in. The three set up a makeshift shelter—still on the mountain ridge, still exposed to the wind and rain. Two of the women, totally exhausted, crawled into their sleeping bags, still wearing their wet clothes. The rain continued to dampen the bags. The other woman was able to recall her survival training. She forced herself to remain awake, eat, drink warm liquids, and keep her bag dry. She descended alone to a lower elevation to get out of the wind. It was too late for the others. Their mental and physical collapse—caused by prolonged exposure to cold intensified by the wetness, wind, and exhaustion—led to stupor, coma, and death during the night. The succession of decisions to reject food, stop in an exposed area, and allow themselves to fall asleep in bags they allowed to become wet led to their deaths.

A number of women reported getting hypothermia, many during cross-country ski trips. One woman was sweaty from hauling herself up an incline on skis. "I made the mistake of getting into my sleeping bag with my damp clothes on. I just couldn't get warm."

One woman descended into an ice cave with a group of teenagers. The girls' wet, tightly clinging jeans and the constant cold temperature of the cave soon took their toll on several of them. As hypothermia set in, they became drowsy and confused. The girls were hauled out by ropes and bundled up for several hours in sleeping bags under the ninety-degree desert sun.

Small, slender women run a greater risk of getting hypothermia than their larger counterparts. Women of the same height and weight as male partners will be less prone because their higher percentage of body fat serves as insulation.

For prevention, stay dry, stay out of the wind, and wear proper protection (wool clothing is especially effective). Hats are important because most heat is lost from the head.

Victims often deny they are in trouble. Believe the symptoms, not what they tell you. If you recognize the symptoms in yourself, ask the group to help you.

The first move must be to stop heat loss and restore body temperature. Seek shelter. If the victim is wet, remove the clothing and put on dry clothes. Have the person crawl into a warm sleeping bag. Warm drinks, even hot water, will restore body heat. If the person is in advanced stages of hypothermia, has quit shivering and is starting to go into a coma, force the person to stay awake. At this point share your body heat. Save a life by removing your clothes and getting into the bag with the victim. Skin-to-skin contact is the most efficient way to transfer body heat.

When camping in the snow, you can construct protection in an emergency by digging a hole in the snow. Lay branches over the hole for a roof, then pile packed snow on the branches. Bore a couple of air holes or your body heat and respiration will cause condensation within the shelter. You can also construct a lean-to of branches or simply station yourself between some boulders and anchor your poncho or tent over the top for a roof. If using a poncho or tent, periodically knock off the snow or water which accumulates. Stay put until the weather clears, and you have a chance of getting out quickly.

Heat Stress

Almost every experienced outdoorswoman can recall hiking a ridge exposed to the sun. No breeze is blowing. Her skin is wet and her shirt is glued to her backpack. Sweat trickles into her eyes and off her nose. Her lips are cracked. She has two-quarts-worth of cotton mouth. Hours pass before she finds shade or breath of breeze. Her goal is still several miles away. Her water supply is rapidly diminishing, and she feels like she's going to die.

If she ignores her condition and presses on without water or rest, she could die. One woman collapsed from heat exhaustion miles away from help. "I practically crawled back, and managed to find some dirty water to drink."

Heat stress happens when the body cannot cope with the excess environmental heat burden. It can happen when you are working or resting, in the glaring sun or under a cloud cover. (4) & (5)

For men, evaporating sweat is one of the body's primary defenses against heat. In women, who do not sweat as profusely as men, the heat regulating mechanism is not so clear and is thought to be more related to the cardiovascular system.

In high humidity, the potential for heat stress is great because the cooling sweat doesn't evaporate as easily and thereby doesn't perform its function as well. When fluids lost through sweating and urination are not replaced, body temperature climbs.

Two types of heat stress disorders can occur. These are heat exhaustion and heat stroke. A third, heat cramps or salt cramps, has an unknown cause but is thought to often be caused by a salt deficiency.

Salt is lost through sweating. One young woman in a group of teenagers hiking in the heat had been on a salt-free diet. When she doubled up in pain, the leader suspected an appendicitis when, in fact, a salt tablet and some liquids were all that she needed.

In specifying salt intake, it is important to realize that the average diet in the United States contains a great deal of salt. Fit, acclimatized people need less salt as their bodies learn some conservation and an overdose of salt can itself cause illness. (6) Salt tablets should not be taken if water is not available. Administration of salt tablets without sufficient liquids can itself cause heat damage.

Heat cramps are best prevented by a generous salting of meals. Commercial trail rations often contain a lot of sodium so this may be all you need. Salt tablets are not suggested unless medical supervision is available or the person has not received salt in her diet.

Heat exhaustion occurs when the blood vessels are so busy cooling the skin that needed blood supplies are drawn from the brain and other vital organs. Dehydration is also believed to reduce the volume of blood, making the problem worse.

Symptoms of heat exhaustion are faintness, rapid heartbeat, weakness, clammy skin, unstable walk, and possible nausea and collapse. A headache may be present. The body temperature will not be above normal; it may be below normal. Sweat and a pale skin color may also be present; however, this varies. Treatment consists of rest in the shade and the intake of liquids. It should not take the victim long to recovery.

Heat stroke comes about very rapidly. It occurs during long bouts in the heat with no relief. The person may earlier have felt very hot, then quickly may become confused, uncoordinated, delirious, or unconscious. Usually the body temperature will be above 105 degrees Farenheit. The skin will be hot and sweating completely absent.

Treatment must be immediate; otherwise brain damage or death will result. Immerse the victim in cold water if possible. Otherwise, cover the person with clothes soaked in water or alcohol to help dissipate the heat. Vigorously massage legs and arms to get the blood circulating. Fanning helps, as does removal of clothing. The person should be moved to the shade.

A persistent coma dictates immediate evacuation. Those who survive heat stroke may develop kidney failure and be intolerant to heat in the future.

The cause of heat stroke is a debated item among researchers. New evidence disputes the idea that heat stroke is caused by the body's failure to produce enought sweat to cool the skin. The sweat rate should not decrease steadily if one drinks sufficient water. The idea that heat stroke is caused by exhaustion of the sweat glands has also been disputed. Although this may sound esoteric, it is important because the old theory implies that women are more susceptible to heat stroke than men because they do not sweat as much.

Heat stress is best avoided by physical training for the work to be performed and by gradual acclimatization (two weeks) to doing that same work in a hot environment. (7) Since the latter is often not practical, reduce your expectations if entering uncustomarily hot areas.

Women with long hair are much cooler if they bind it in braids. Hats are also important. Dunking your head in a cool stream; taking off your shirt and wetting it in cool water; and moistening a bandanna to wipe your forehead, neck, and wrists are good measures. Drink lots of liquids, more than you are thirsty for. Do not wear binding or restrictive clothing. Rubber reducing belts and other items sold for weight control should never be used, because they retard the body's ability to regulate heat. Do not take diuretics such as caffeine which cause you to urinate frequently.

Rest in the shade when the sun is at its zenith. Like animals, you may have to travel at night and early morning and late afternoon hours. Night travel requires a flashlight or good moon and knowledge of the trail and of which animals may be about and their habits.

Vegetation

Skinny-dipping in a slow, undulating river is a joy that is a reminder of Tom Sawyer's day. But that lovely vegetation reflecting off the water may be of the poison variety. Poison oak, ivy, and sumac are the three witches of the plant world and have the ability to put an exposed person into the hospital. The usual result of contact with these plants is swelling, red sores, and localized itching. Some people react with violent rashes and swelling, pus, and dangerously high fevers. It is unknown why some people react more violently than others to the oil in the plants. Sometimes a person goes for years without exhibiting any reaction whatsoever and suddenly she has a severe

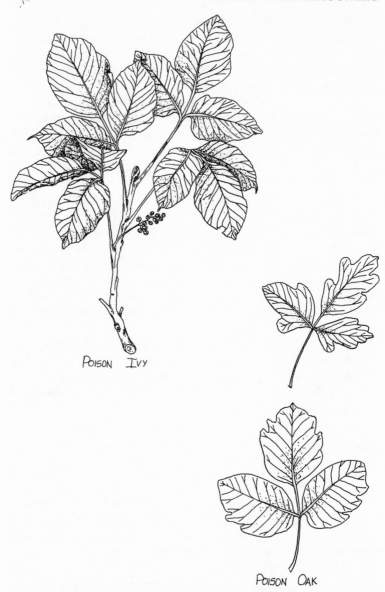

POISON IVY

POISON OAK

Poison ivy and poison oak always have three leaflets. Poison ivy grows everywhere in the United States except California. Its leaves are glossy and it can take the form of a small plant, vine, or shrub. Poison oak grows in California and adjacent states. It appears mostly in a shrub form but can be a vine.

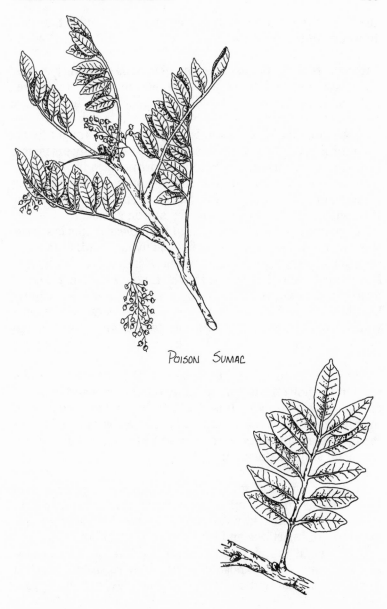

POISON SUMAC

Poison sumac grows in the eastern United States. It is a woody shrub or small tree.

case. There are immunization treatments, although they are time-consuming and never guaranteed to be 100 percent effective.

Recognize these plants. They are ubiquitous and vary in size and appearance according to locale, elevation, sun exposure, and presence of water. They change color with the seasons. They are very beautiful in the autumn—and treacherous.

As a young child in Rhode Island, a woman brought home a beautiful bouquet of autumn leaves that she proudly presented to her mother. The leaves were placed in a vase in the living room for everyone to admire. A few hours later her mother could no longer see and her face had swollen to twice its normal size. She had to be hospitalized for poison sumac.

The poisonous chemical *urushiol* from these plants is spread about by hot water rather than removed by it. The oil from these plants also remains in your clothing. Handle these with care. If you are constantly in areas in which you will be exposed to these plants, keep your whole body covered, wash thoroughly, handle your clothing carefully, and don't wipe your face with your hands. Sleep in a separate change of clothes. When going to the bathroom, watch out for the vegetation brushing your derriere.

The Russian River in California was the culprit when one woman got poison oak rash not only on her arms and face, but on more personal parts. It is next to impossible not to scratch the blisters because they itch so much. After agonizing through the day determined not to scratch, she found she'd done so in her sleep and the poison had spread.

If you have exposed only a small area, you may not need to treat it. A cool, mild solution of salt and water helps relieve the itching as does calamine lotion or mud. A really tough bout will have to be treated with steroid ointment; disabling doses may require injections and tablets over a period of days.

Don't get in the way of the smoke of burning poison oak, sumac, or ivy. Such exposure is one of the easiest ways to get a severe case that will affect your whole body, especially your eyes.

One woman, a backcountry firefighter who knew this awesome trio very well and who avoided it just as well, spent one evening brushing and hugging her neighbor's dog. Two days later she had to visit a skin specialist in the emergency room of a hospital so she could see again. She had developed a bad case of poison oak rash by handling the dog.

Stinging nettles are the curse of the outdoorswoman in the humid East. These scratchy plants grow quickly to Olympic sizes in many places. Wearing two cotton, long-sleeved shirts, and heavy, loose pants will help protect you. Relief is usually found from cold water, calamine lotion, mud, or time away from the plants.

In the desert, there is no lack of catus. Momma cacti are very fruitful so baby cacti dot the landscape. Catus can penetrate your boot easily if the spikes make contact at the right angle. Even more annoying, the small cacti cling to your socks and pants.

Thick clumps of chaparral, a community of plants found in semiarid country, are almost impossible to penetrate. In search of Indian cave paintings, one woman spent an entire day crawling on her knees and stomach through chaparral. Almost at the cave, gulping air in the hot density of the chaparral, she came across some very old sunglasses and a film container. Some other fool had the same idea and had taken the same path. She never found the paintings and looked in more accessible places after that. After all, if the Indians went to such trouble to hide their paintings, perhaps the secrets should be kept hidden.

There are other plants that are hazardous to the wilderness traveler, particularly if you're thinking about adding them to your meal. Get to know plants, such as miner's lettuce or mushrooms, very well before inviting them to dinner.

Insects

Insects have their place in nature; however, their place and your place are not usually compatible. Like shifts in weather and availability of water, they are not something the city dweller gives much thought to. Do not slight them by disregarding their possible presence. Always take a strong no-nonsense insect repellent, protective clothing, and possibly mosquito netting or a tent. In addition to covering every exposed inch of your body with insect repellent, repellent in a liquid or spray can be applied to your clothing. As an added deterrent, put repellent in the hair, and a double dose around the ears, neck, and hairline. On a warm, humid night, insect repellent is not a panacea. Not all insects respect it, and the repellent will make you feel hotter as it collects in your pores. This adage is especially true in the humid climate of the South where it is almost required to carry a net or tent for sanity.

One time in the Escalante River canyon, Slim Woodruff drove up to find a hidden triple arch. She located the trailhead and climbed down for a day hike. Since it was just for the day, she left both her long pants and her insect repellent (packed in her first aid kit) behind. In the canyon bottom, she was assaulted by hundreds of biting deerflies. She couldn't move without being literally covered by them. She dove into the river and laid under the water to escape them. Then she sloshed her way upstream to find the arches. "Every single time I leave my first aid kit behind, I regret it one way or the other," she says. On the way back out, she cut tamarisk branches and tied them to her waist so they would brush her exposed legs and help keep the flies off. "But some of them followed me all the way to the rim."

You can discourage an onsalught of ants by laying your tarp on the ground and centering yourself and your pack in the middle. By applying the insect repellent around the edge of the tarp, a barrier can be formed.

Mosquitoes can be thick enough that a person actually cannot breathe without inhaling them. They are warm weather friends and frequent moist areas. Something as innocent as an alpine stream can harbor them. Mysteriously, some people are more attractive to mosquitoes than others. It has been found that dark-colored clothing is more attractive than light-colored clothing. Certain shampoos, lotions, and perfumes may also guide them to you.

Since mosquitoes require stagnant water and warm weather to hatch, they are less likely to be present if temperatures have recently dropped below freezing and if you do not camp near standing water. If you can hold out until the evening coldness settles in with the night, the mosquitoes will disappear. A wind or breeze also discourages mosquitoes.

Myrna Ahlgren, a public information technician for Voyagers National Park in Minnesota, said blackflies and mosquitoes were a real problem when she was camping one spring in the northern lakes area. She and her husband had only a tarp to sleep under and the insects made a feast of them.

Another woman encountered flies so thick that she could not see well. A straw hat with long fringes and a bandanna constantly swatting the flies, along with protective clothing, helped her survive the ordeal in better comfort than others in the party. When she laid down to sleep at night (the flies mercifully withdrew at sunset), she would close her eyes and still see all the black bodies darting in front of her. The only places for relief during the whole trip were far out on the snow of glacier fields, windy ridges, an ice cave, and lying submerged in a cold mountain stream, as the group had not taken a tent.

Chiggers are the bane of eastern wetland explorers. These insects crawl along the lower leg, especially near the socks and boot edges. Their bite leaves an itch that you can wear your nails out on. Heat and perspiration increase the irritation and encourage the creatures to dig in. Cold water, calamine lotion, and cool mud help provide relief.

Ticks are flat little guys with eight legs which can transmit several diseases, the most notable being Rocky Mountain Spotted Fever. Most ticks do not carry diseases, and if found early enough, can be removed before they bury their heads in your flesh.

The old remedy of removing embedded ticks with a hot match to make them back out has been supplemented with the antidote of smothering them in oil for one-half hour, then pulling them out with tweezers.

Ticks are interested in blood and wherever it is closest to the surface are likely places to look. These include the bra and panty lines, along with belt line, behind the ears, the hairline, scalp, and pubic and underarm hair.

Light-colored clothing makes them easier to spot. Checks for ticks should be done about every ten minutes in areas of thick vegetation. A very thorough check, in the flesh, should be done before retiring to make sure that freckles and moles are just freckles and moles. Inspect your clothing and gear along with your body when you get home. Once they implant themselves, they feel much like a bump or mole on the surface of the skin.

Occasionally ticks can strike in difficult places. One woman had to seek a doctor to have a tick removed from her inner ear. Another had to have one removed from her labium. And another had to have a tick removed from the depths of a swollen, infected belly button.

The pajahello tick, known in the Southwest, can paralyze its victim. This tick moves so slowly that the prey has to lie still for awhile to give the tick time to cling to the body. A wilderness patrolwoman tells of finding a family of backpackers in tears. It seemed that their dog had mysteriously lost the use of her legs overnight. She helped everyone readjust their equipment, carrying a large amount of it on her own back, and helped them place the 70-pound dog in the teenage son's backpack. It turned out that the dog had received the unwelcome bite of the pajahello tick which the vet immediately found and removed. The dog recovered within an hour.

Snakes

Death and serious injury from poisonous snakebite is rare in the United States. Young children, the elderly, and those in poor physical condition are most susceptible to harm. Backcountry users can keep the statistics low by taking a few precautions.

There are only four types of poisonous snakes in the United States: rattlesnake, water moccasin (cottonmouth), copperhead, and coral snake. The first three have the characteristic triangular head, slit pupils, heavy bodies, obvious fangs, and pits between their nostrils and eyes. The coral snake is the anomaly among poisonous snakes with a slender body and head, round eyes, small fangs, and no pits. It can be distinguished from similar-looking harmless species by the presence of yellow bands in addition to red, and possibly black bands coloring its body.

The rattlesnake is the most common in the United States having a territory that extends from east to west, usually in the semiarid and arid regions. The water moccasin lives in the marshy lowlands of southeastern United States. The copperhead is found in swampy, wooded, and rocky areas of the central and eastern United States. The coral snake inhabits primarily the southeast with one rare species in Arizona.

All snakes are intolerant to extremes in heat and cold, and being cold-blooded are more active when it is warm. They frequent areas where they can hide from airborne predators.

Most snakebits occur on the legs, ankles, and hands. When traveling in snake country, keep alert for them on the ground, and use a hiking stick in dense vegetation to warn them of your progress. Always step on top of a log or rock you cannot see over. When climbing, reconnoiter handholds with a stick to avoid surprising a snake lolling there. Always check out a cave before entering. Wear protective boots and clothing.

Snakes do not strike without provocation. If you step on them they will strike. Self preservation is a living creature's natural response, and in spite of its poison, a snake should not be killed unless there is no alternative. If you encounter a snake, move slowly away from it, as sudden motions are threatening.

Treatment for snakebites should be immediate. There are two methods. The first is the "do nothing" approach in which the injured area is subjected to cold (such as a ice pack or immersion) to prevent the poison from spreading. The second is making ⅛ to ¼ inch incisions over the punctures to draw out the poison by bleeding and suction. Advocates of both methods agree that the injured area should be lowered below the heart and that the person should not move unnecessarily. A badly injured person should be evacuated.

The second method is the one which should probably be used if the afflicted person is obviously very sick or has received multiple bites from different snakes or one very large snake. This method should also be used if the person is susceptible, due to physical condition, to the poison.

The second method should be approached with great caution since delicate tendons, nerve endings, and major blood vessels can be severed in the process. Infections and lifelong scarring can result. Consequently, gauge whether the severity of the bite justifies such dramatic action.

Sterilize the injured area, and use a sterile instrument to make the incision. Do not use your mouth for suction if you have open sores through which the venom can enter. Swallowing the venom won't hurt you. A restrictive band placed above the area of swelling will abate the spread of the poison through the subcutaneous tissue. At no time should the band stop the blood flow since the more you restrict the blood flow the more the injured person risks the loss of limb from gangrene. In addition to the sterile knife, make sure the injured area is clean.

Wildlife

We hesitate to place encounters with wildlife in a chapter on the perils of wilderness travel since for most of the women we surveyed, this is one of the principal reasons for going. In our survey, a striking majority felt women were more tender toward animals than men and that this is good. Bev Cochrane said, "All encounteres with wildlife are burned in my memory; mink, moose, geese, deer, a young bear, a baby loon, eagle, osprey, a coyote pup."

But wildlife is, after all, wild life—unpredictable, occasionally aggressive, and in need of much territory. Always give wildlife distance and the right-of-way. Their definition of a violation of space may be very broad; with some grizzlies it can be as much as two hundred yards. (8)

"Never corner or surprise a large animal," says Katherine Bridwell-Bos. "Even a deer can be deadly when frightened. The mutual curiosity will often allow you closer contact with large animals, but don't appear too interested. Pretend to be going about your business." Katherine adds, for example, that wild stallions may turn on you, and that she was followed for three hours by a large antelope buck.

One woman's experience bears out one of Katherine's points. Upon encountering a mother moose and calf not five feet away, she stopped casually. She calmly got out her camera as if she weren't aware the pair were near her. When she turned to take the picture, the mother regarded her with some suspicion. "It's

PRONGHORN (ANTELOPE)

okay," she told her. "I'm just going to take your picture." The
mother returned to her browsing and eventually got bored
enough with the photographer to quit watching her.

Stopping to take pictures is not advisable if the animal has
determined that you are a threat. "I was severely chastized by
a surly badger in Canada once when I was walking down a
woodland trail alone," says Mary Grisco, a psychologist. "When
we saw each other we both stopped. I began to circle. It barraged
me with belligerent chatter and proceeded to advance. It went
through this routine—advance, sit up and scold, advance, sit
up and scold, several times before I realized that I was the
intruder. As I turned, it started to chase me."

Dr. Mary Meagher, director of biological research for Yellowstone National Park, who has lived seasonally in isolated wilderness for twenty years and is one of the country's leading

grizzly bear experts, believes that bears attack if they sense you are frightened. As with Mary Grisco's experience with the badger, it is better not to turn your back. Back away slowly. Talking to wild animals in a low, calm voice is advocated by Bradford Angier, author of *How to Stay Alive in the Woods* (Macmillan Books, 1958).

If they feel threatened, most animals will attack to protect territory or their young, or will make an escape.

Most wild animals are most dangerous during their mating seasons. Bear mothers with small offspring are often the most dangerous because they wish to protect their small cubs.

In looking out for wildlife, get to know what they eat and where they sleep. Moose, for example, are found among willows in marshy areas where they munch the succulent plants. Bears are found where succulent plants, grubs, and rodents are most abundant. They follow the ripening of spring up the mountain, and in the summer frequent high alpine meadows where snow-melt is just bringing the country into fruition. Berry patches in fruit are likely places as are avalanche chutes where the pickings along the tree line are good.

Most animals are active at dusk and after dark. In genuine wilderness, this is not a good time for wandering. Many bear attacks on sleeping campers have been just before dawn. Fishermen are often approached by bears, so good fishing areas in known bear country are also likely places. If you were a large omnivore who had to constantly roam the country-side in order to fill your belly, would you hunt down an elusive deer or go for the carcass of an animal which died during the winter? If there is a dead animal near your campsite, move far way from the odor.

Get to know and look for wildlife signs. Stream crossings, lake shores, and wet sand are good places to find tracks. If you get good enough, like the late Olaus Murie (9), you can even tell how fast the animal is moving and how recent the passage by examining the tracks. Most bears, wolves, and other predators are creatures of habit. They do have a particular territory. If you find a den, it's time to move on—likely the bear will return. Other signs are scats and, with bears, claw marks dug into trees.

The first trails in the wilderness were laid down by the animals. Animals use trails for the same reason we do. It's easier. They also frequent the same water sources and like to sleep in similar places—protected from the elements and out of the wind.

If you see a neatly padded area atop an inviting bed of pine needles, look close around the site. If you see animal droppings nearby, you may be taking someone's bed.

Although an adult elk is a magnificantly strong animal, you'll be lucky to ever see one. Hear them, yes. See thousands of their tracks around the only lake for miles, but see one? This is why an elk trophy says more for a hunter's ability than a deer rack, or even a moose rack.

Cougars may stalk a person, but attacks are next to zero. Unless you are a wildlife biologist who seeks cougar, you'll probably never see one.

Grizzly and moose are kings of the wilds and seem to know it. A moose will usually just stand there and stare at you or charge. Hiding behind a tree will usually suffice since the moose will forget what it was charging at.

One man staked his tent in a broad meadow, far into country not marked by trails or guidebooks. Long about dusk, a bull moose came down to inspect what he'd apparently decided was his meadow. He stood at the other end of the meadow and protested. He stomped, scuffled, and did a few half charges, then shook his massive head in disgust and anger. He left in a huff but returned several times later. He finally gave up.

Bears are the most dangerous wildlife in the western world. However, while a healthy respect tinged with fear is reasonable, the destructive nonsense of the B-grade movie *Grizzly* is not. Statistically, the chance of being mauled is about .00007 percent, or one attack per 1.5 million visitors. (10)

The harm that comes to backpackers and other campers from bears is the result of two things. The first and foremost is habitat loss. As civilization closes in on them with summer home developments, mining and timber extractions, and ski resorts, it systematically destroys their range. As people corner them into smaller and smaller reservations, they are bound to run into them since the bear has nowhere else to go.

The second danger comes from contact with humans by which the animal learns to associate us with food. A wild bear is turned into a rogue bear by garbage and feeding by humans. Injured and older bears, unable to forage as well, may be more likely to frequent campgrounds or roust humans for food. Although the National Park Service insists that everyone camp at designated sites, some backcountry users refuse to do this because the developed sites are probably the first place a wayward bear would look for food. It's not cute to feed a wild bear. Doing so may ultimately bring about its death.

Grizzly bears were classified as threatened in 1974 in the United States under the Endangered Species Act. Consequently, it is illegal to hunt them in most places. It is not hunting pressure that has diminished the grizzly population, but habitat loss. Limited hunts would probably be beneficial since, as Dr. Charles Jonkel, a research associate for the Montana Forest and Conservation Station at the University of Montana, says, "hunted grizzlies become wary, avoiding man and areas frequented by him; this reduces conflict by decreasing the corruption of the bears' natural behavior." (11)

Most reported bear encounters are in National Parks. The reason given is because park bears are more accustomed to humans and because hunting in National Parks has historically been prohibited.

Most bears do not consider people good eating. Even among the few that have killed people, it has generally not been as a food source. Among grizzlies, there are some exceptions. Some grizzlies have consumed portions of their victims.

Often a bear will approach simply to make out what you are. It can't see very well. It's sense of hearing is about that of a human's and its sense of smell is very acute.

The National Park Service and United States Forest Service have printed a brochure titled "Grizzly, Grizzly, Grizzly" which admonishes women to stay out of grizzly country during their menstrual flow. Some officials assert that percentage wise, more women than men are attacked by bears. These assertations are not backed up by published research. One study was recently conducted with polar bears that showed they equated used tampons with seal remains (their natural prey) as preferred foods. The polar bears were not attracted to the smell of blood, but specifically to menstrual blood. However, a polar bear is not a grizzly bear. Polar bears are carnivores and have been known to hunt humans. They are the most predatory of the predators. Grizzly bears are omnivores and generally fill their stomachs with berries, plants, insects, and small rodents. They do not require a full-time red meat diet.

Before the polar bear studies, the assumption that women are in more danger during menses was apparently based on one incident in Glacier National Park in which one young woman was menstruating when she was attacked. This woman was wearing a sanitary napkin, not a tampon, and the park service report of the death speculated that the bear could smell the menstrual odor. Since tampons are worn internally, if a woman is careful about hygiene and frequently changes, burns, or stores used tampons in airtight bags, the bear will have much less chance of detecting the odor. If you have a heavy menstrual flow, you may want to suppress your period entirely while in grizzly country by taking birth control pills continuously for the duration of the trip.

Those who hold to the idea that women are attacked more frequently than men think that it could be due to the odors of perfumed toiletries. One researcher uses perfume to attract the bears so he can study them. Again, there is no statistical evidence that women are attacked more than men.

The grizzly brochure also states that sexual activity may attract bears. If this is true, it is the presence of the odor that is implicated, and the danger is most likely during the bear's mating season of June and early July. Keep your body, clothing, sleeping bag, campsite, and clothing free of odor.

Some research is being done on the presence of phermones, sexual attractant smells emitted by animals, in the human female as a reason why bears might be attracted to her (if they are). If phermones are the attractant, they are strange indeed since many attacks on women have been by female grizzly bears. Furthermore, phermones are not known to operate on an interspecies level.

This issue has equal employment opportunity implications for women in the field. Menses could be used as a reason to keep a woman out of the field, thereby not allowing her to acquire the experience necessary to advance on an equal footing with male collegues. Women have been attacked while menstruating, but the question is cause or coincidence, as one female forest service employee says. Although the factor of menses is plausible, no one asked if male odors (phermones, sweat, semen) are the cause when men are attacked.

The grizzly's range is generally limited to Wyoming, Montana, Alaska, Idaho, Alberta, British Columbia, and the Yukon and Northwest Territories. One was encountered recently in Colorado. If entering grizzly country, ask for specific information on bear sightings, which are reported and recorded. Insist on accurate information, not someone's guess. If you are deeply concerned, write ahead of time to the managing agency before planning your trip. Park service employees have been accused of being overly casual about grizzlies and not providing users with a reasonable appraisal of the danger. (12) Information about bear sightings and frequency is not generally available to the public. This may be caused by oversight or the fear that if the information was widely distributed, tourists would seek the bears out. You may have to be insistent to acquire the detailed data.

Animals are likely to detect the presence of bears before you do. For example, most horses will show signs of stress long before you notice anything. Vicki Montgomery encountered a black bear in Alaska while camping. She was peacefully ensconced in her tent when her cat became very alert. He walked to the tent opening and looked out. He registered a look on his face she says could only be described as incredulous. Vicki peered out and saw the bear. The cat made for the nearest tree, while Vicki waited in the tent. Eventually the bear went away.

Be alert for bears on the trail. Make noise so you don't accidentally surprise one. Bells worn suspended so they constantly tinkle are a good solution as is hiking with a group. Groups of four or more persons are rarely attacked. One woman surprised a grizzly while jogging on a Yellowstone Park trail. She tried to run away from it and is now undergoing plastic surgery. Another woman was hiking alone and came upon a grizzly. She backed off and found another route, but the animal

AMERICAN BLACK BEAR

GRIZZLY BEAR

circled and attacked her anyway. She too survived but had to
undergo extensive surgery. A grizzly can outrun a racehorse.

Someday, sometime, as Mary Meagher says, you may meet
up with the wrong bear. That's a chance you take. Upon an
encounter, stand your ground and back away slowly. Calm talking may help. Unfasten your pack waist belt. Discard your pack
if the bear seems ready to pursue. It's likely the food in the
pack will be more interesting than you. Keep backing off. If a
tree is nearby, climb it. (Can you?) If all of these fail, go into
a fetal position with your hands around your neck to protect
the spinal cord and tuck in your elbows and knees to protect
your intestines, lungs and throat. Lie perfectly still and don't
cry out. Most likely the bear will push you about and may
possibly bite you, then leave. If the animal keeps coming back
and inflicting injury, only you can determine whether action
on your part will save your life. In one incident, the woman
didn't make any noise although the bear was hurting her. Finally she cried out and this discouraged the bear long enough
that she had time to crawl to her pack, which contained a two-
way radio. As she radioed for help, the delay caused by the
noise she made deterred the bear long enough for the helicopter
to arrive which frightened the bear away.

Other last ditch preventatives are loud noises (firecrackers,
whistles, the bark of a gun), a flare, and chemical repellent. The
repellent of the trade name Halt, (13) used by postal workers
to stop dogs, has also been used with success. (14) The spray
must be directed at the animal's face and eyes from no less than
ten feet. It temporarily subdues the bear for up to five minutes.

Large caliber guns make a lot of noise and if aimed at the
ground in front of the animal will kick up a lot of dust. You'd
better be a good shot if you plan to down a grizzly with a gun.
One Glacier National Park ranger says to aim for the shoulder
joint to immobilize a bear's advance. If you miss, you've got an
enraged bear. If one attacks you at close range, aim for the
jugular vein, temple, or between the eyes. A small caliber gun,
such as a .22, won't do it. During an encounter in Colorado, a
man saved himself by stabbing the attacking animal repeatedly
in the neck with a razor-sharp, sturdy hunting arrow.

It is illegal to carry an operable gun in national parks. You can be ticketed and fined if the gun is not dismantled. A dismantled gun is not the same as one that is not loaded. The gun must be literally taken apart so you won't be suspected of illegally hunting in a game preserve.

In camp, sleep at least two hundred feet upwind from your cooking and food storage area. Hang food and odorous items in a tree. Wash up before going to bed; this includes removing insect repellent. Do not wear the clothing you cooked in to bed. Do not keep food and other odorous items in your tent. Burn all fish entrails and keep your camp scrupulously clean. Clean up spills and drain dishwater in to the fire. Locate your sleeping area near a tree that you can climb. Plan your escape route and make sure the tree is tall and sturdy enough that you can escape the bear. You need to be ten to twelve feet up the tree for the bear not to be able to reach you. One man lost part of his buttock because he was not able to get high enough. Do not camp near a den, game trail, or water source. Keep something nearby with which to make noise. You can also leave your cook kit and other metal items out to alert you should an investigating bear wander into camp and stumble over them. If you see warnings about bears posted on trailheads, stay out. Camp in another area, not at the posted trailhead. A sign only got there because more than one person was troubled, a bear has been especially aggressive, or there have been several sightings.

If you should be harmed, you can demand the bear's head as a price, but think about it. Often, more than one bear is destroyed before the offending bear is located. Often no one knows for sure if the right bear has been killed. Further, was the harm that came to you your own fault? Did you drain tuna fish oil on the ground in your camp? Were you wandering about at night? Did you follow a path littered with fresh bear scat? Did you camp near a water hole or game trail? Did you surprise the bear? Did you come between a mother and her cubs? Did you bring an untrained dog with you which could disturb a bear and bring it running back to you?

The hazards of the wilderness, including bear encounters, are real enough and should not be minimized or overlooked. But, as Slim Woodruff says, she feels much safer in the woods than in the city. "I worked one summer with kids from the New

York ghettos. They were agog at the thought that I came from the wild and woolly west. They couldn't understand how I could go into the trackless waste and face snakes, spiders, wolves, and Indians. I, on the other hand, couldn't understand how *they* could daily face the perils of Spanish Harlem."

Little Red Riding Hood

A fifth-generation descendant of Davy Crockett says that the Appalachian Trail has become so dangerous he'd sooner stroll through Harlem at midnight than hike it. David Crockett, a district attorney in Tennessee, says he knows of no cases where men were molested, but thinks any woman or group of women who walk this or any other wilderness trail unescorted is asking for trouble.

"I will state that in fourteen years of management of the Appalachian Trail and other trails located from Georgia to Virginia within the National Forest, I have known of only a few unpleasant incidents with women in backcountry situations," says B. D. Barr, Watauga District ranger of the Cherokee National Forest headquartered in Cleveland, Tennessee.

Other land managers contacted nationally, such as David F. McAllister, a law enforcement officer for the Rocky Mountain Region of the National Park Service, said the incidence of violent crimes was relatively low within the forty-one parks in that region.

John Orr, a forest supervisor speaking for the Ouachita and Ozark–St. Francis National Forests, reported no incidents of violent crimes against female users. Others, such as the Pacific Northwest Region of the National Park Service, said that the crime rate has been holding steady since 1977, while still others reported both upward and downward trends.

The incidence of crime has grown with the increase of users of federal recreation areas, according to a report to Congress from the Comptroller General in 1977.

"I would say there has been an increase in crime against persons of about 100 percent since 1960," says one park police captain. "However, 80 percent of this increase has come since large city parks were included in the National Park system in the mid-1970s."

Clearly, such varied responses suggest that the degree of danger for women in the backcountry varies with geographical location and the perception of the observer. Of the women surveyed, most had gone on backcountry trips alone. About one-quarter did express some concern over the possibility of violence. About 43 percent of them felt that a woman may have more to fear than men in a wilderness situation. "Not from the wilderness itself, but possibly from human intruders," said Nelle Tobias, a leading Idaho conservationist and retired mountain resort operator.

On National Park Service land, which receives the highest percentage of visitors outside of reservoirs managed by the Army Corps of Engineers, the probability of being raped, according to 1978 figures, was one per every 4,348,000 visitors. In contrast, rape probability according to the Federal Bureau of Investigation's 1978 Uniform Crime Reports was one per 1,389 females in metropolitan areas. On National Park Service land, there were 91 rapes in 1978 and twelve criminal homicides. Again, contrast this with FBI figures for the same year of 67,131 rapes and 19,555 murders nationally.

Circumstances surrounding crime in federal recreation areas were summed up by Carl R. Holmberg, a law enforcement specialist for the Southwest Region of the National Park Service. "It is our analysis that crime occurs more frequently in areas receiving the most dense visitation; campgrounds and parking lots being the areas of most incidents. We do not believe that the backcountry areas are as prone to visitation by those persons who are inclined toward criminal activity.

"The victims of the incidents of rape . . . mainly occurred in parks situated near urban areas where the persons involved met, or the victim was abducted outside the park and driven into the park where the crime took place," Holmberg says. He adds that one attempted rape and murder occurred with a couple who were abducted while hitchhiking.

"The backcountry is usually out-of-the-way of the criminal element," says Bill McDonald, a law enforcement specialist for the Southwest Region of the National Park Service. "There's

not a lot of opportunity for a rapist to be successful in the
wilderness. He would stick to a place were there are a lot of
women and where they would be easy to get to. In addition, in
National Parks it's too easy to catch a rapist. The Big Bend
National Park, for example, has only two entries. All we'd have
to do is seal them off."

McDonald's reasoning is confirmed by the facts that 71 percent of all rapes are planned and that a majority occur in the
home. (15)

The occurrence of violent crimes against women is substantially less in the backcountry or in developed recreation sites
than in urbanized areas. However, this should not create a false
sense of security, says Jeannette M. Nish, a landscape architect
for the George Washington National Forest, headquartered in
Virginia.

Women have been sexually harassed in the backcountry. "I
was out canoeing alone when a male hiker grabbed my canoe
and would not let go. Although I was dirty and scraggly, this
didn't put him off. He rationalized that he hadn't seen a woman
in two weeks. He also claimed that he was a Tennessee stud.
I didn't try to use force to escape him. I just talked and talked.
After twenty minutes he finally let go and I paddled away."
She adds that she fears this most in the backcountry and is
always cautious around men who use "easy access" such as
packstrings, and off-road vehicles. "Camping by them always
seems to invite intense and undressing stares."

Another woman said that her friend was accosted and physically bothered while working as a wilderness ranger in Oregon.
Another said that two male guests (during different trips) had
tried to make an advance while she was alone with them. "I
just strong-armed them off and didn't hear any more about it."

Many suggestions were given for ways to avoid and confront
rape and aggression. "The only advice I can give would be to
check with officials and determine where the problem areas are
and avoid them," wrote David Wilson, Nolichucky District
ranger for the Cherokee National Forest. Others noted that the
incidents on the Appalachian Trail had taken place in areas
which abut private land and arterial roads.

Camp off the trail and not near developed sites, where it

would be obvious that you are alone. Pretend not to be alone. Indicate that your husband or boyfriend is nearby with a group of defensive linemen from the Los Angeles Rams. Inquire loudly if the size thirteen hiking boots you gave him are holding up on the trail. Complain to overly inquisitive strangers that your husband is so violent that you must take frequent trips into the wilderness to calm him down.

If you feel threatened, befriend a family if one is camped nearby. Of course, being married or someone's uncle or brother doesn't make a man trustworthy, but the presence of his family will mitigate questionable intentions. Don't camp near groups of unattached men.

"Be six feet tall and develop an icy stare," says Virginia Bailey. "Be civil, but cool," says another woman. "Look purposeful and as tough as possible," said another. "It helps to have thought about what to do in advance," says Mary Griffith, an outdoorswoman in Maine. "Think positively and know self defense," says Lindi Wall, an expedition leader and driver for Encounter Overland whose trips take her deep into the backcountry of Asia and Africa.

Slim Woodruff, who knows self defense, loves to tell of her first evening in an outdoor education center where she worked one fall. "I was walking down a dark road when one of the male staff members tried to scare me. He lept out of the bushes and made a grab for me, but I was not in the least startled. Rather than screaming or even feeling a lurch of the stomach, I affected a wide-legged stance, hands ready to grab him back, and let loose with a loud karate yell. He immediately reported that I had tried to take his head off, and I was labeled as a tough "libbie" who the boys should not mess with. I knew all the time that he was only kidding, but was rather proud of myself. I felt sure, had he really intended to drag me into the bushes, that I could have fought him off."

One of the incidents in Tennessee which Crockett was so upset about is interesting in light of the response of the women. In one newspaper account, two women were stopped on the trail by some boys carrying a shotgun who said they were going to rape them. "The women pleaded with them for awhile and finally, one grabbed the shotgun out of the boy's hand and like to bent it around his neck," Crockett reportedly said. "They took the boys' car and drove it down to the sheriff's office. Lucky for them they were dealing with juveniles."

Such a feat would be harder to pull off with a grown man, but the teenagers will probably think twice before trying to harass another woman. It is worth noting that 54 percent of the forcible rape arrests in 1978 were of males under the age of twenty-five, 33 percent were under twenty-one years old, and 16 percent were under age eighteen. The largest concentration is in the sixteen-to-twenty-four age range. "The typical American perpetrator of forcible rape is little more than an aggressive, hostile youth who chooses to do violence to women." (16) Most rapes are also perpetrated by more than one individual. (17)

Crockett's warning that women shouldn't enter the backcountry alone can be disagreed with as can one forest supervisor who does not allow women to go into the field alone. As with keeping women out of the field because of the bear attacks, such prohibitions have equal employment opportunity implications. Although it is well known that most violent crime is perpetrated by men against men, rather than in other combinations, this fact is not used as a reason to limit and protect men or to keep them out of the field.

Always going with a group or partner is not practical for the active outdoorswoman. Often such partners are hard to find. The positive experiences of being alone, such as peace, confidence, independence, and privacy, should not be denied to women. There are risks, but in terms of crime, they are much less than in the city. The less women view themselves and behave as if they are prey, the less uninformed men will continue to approach them as such.

An example of a passive attitude that reinforces negative stereotypes is a group of thirteen women who were snow camping when two men on snowmobiles approached the camp at night. The men called out to campers, who were all lodged in their tents. The women waited in shuddering silence for the snowmobilers to go away. After calling out several times, the men finally became angry and drove away. What were the women afraid of? Why didn't they go out to meet the men? They outnumbered them. The men may have been lost, had an injured companion, or have been in need of food or shelter. It is highly unlikely that an armed desperado would be making an escape from the posse in the dead of winter on a snowmobile. Even so, the snowmobilers had no way of knowing whether or not the campers were armed.

Should women carry guns or other defensive weapons? They regularly carry chemical sprays in the city, why not in the backcountry? Guns are trickier. It would not be pleasant to see hordes of backpackers all armed to the teeth trekking through the backcountry. However, in remote areas, a pistol on your hip can be a deterrent. It is remarkable how the attitude of strangers changes when they notice the firearm. Of course, you should know how to use it and be sure enough of yourself that it could not be taken away from and used against you.

Rather than resorting to the use of weapons, being cautious is a better solution. Don't make friends too easily. It is naive to assume that just because someone can lace up a pair of hiking boots means that his intentions are honorable. It is probably true that hikers rarely bother other hikers, but there are exceptions. A dog is of little value, other than as a watchdog, unless trained for attack and large enough to do some damage.

If you are bothered, report it. From a law enforcement officer's point of view, all crimes or attempted crimes should be reported so the officer can make a case for funding for more personnel in the field, and of course, to apprehend the criminal.

If you are a professional, you will have to decide whether or not to report the incident. You know your supervisor's attitude best, and whether or not this will be used as a reason to keep you at a desk.

Women have been sexually harassed by male colleagues while in the field. And there is an understandable reluctance to talk about it, let alone report it. Talking to other trustworthy women is one method of learning how to avoid and confront such problems. It's also a way of giving the offender a well-deserved bad reputation.

To backtrack somewhat, the crimes that are most likely to occur in the backcountry or developed sites are crimes against property—primarily your vehicle. This is termed "car clouting." "We are constantly working on new methods to combat this type of crime," says Lloyd Hill, captain for the National Park police in the Pacific Northwest Region.

Don't leave valuables in your car. Do not leave a note on the windshield announcing your return date. Mark your gear with indelible ink or an engraving. Keep gear out of sight while away from camp. If in a congested area, ask a nearby group to keep an eye on your camp while you do the same for them.

Make your car somewhat more theft proof by taking out the coil wire (ask a mechanic how to do it) so it won't start and by attaching a device which locks the steering wheel to the gas pedal. Newer models are harder to steal than older ones because of the safety features (locking steering wheel) which are included in their design. In addition, try to park the car so it is not visible from the road if in a remote area. In heavily used areas, park the car near others so a thief won't be sure if the owner is nearby or not. Better yet, park near a ranger station and tell the ranger when you expect to return.

In closing, by pointing out the perils, it is hoped that you will be prepared for your own and won't need some hero to bail you out. He may not be there.

7

Trail Companions

IN AN ACCOUNT written in 1905 by Marion Randall, an early Sierra Club member and one of the club's best writers, the "girls" automatically assumed the role of serving dinner. In other essays absent-minded men thrust out cups to the ladle-bearing ladies without bothering to acknowledge their presence. In others the virtues of the male leadership and guides are extolled, and women are credited for not being weaklings.

Eight years later, it's easy to smugly report to these women that they were seen as sweet servants and companions, while women today are of independent means and minds. But not only are women indeed indebted to these forerunners, but they continue to be plagued by the male and female roles described by society.

Male and Female Roles

Why, after a group has hiked all day, should the woman prepare dinner while the man goes fishing? Why should he be the carrier and reader of the maps, the firebuilder, and the one who sets up the tent? Chances are that he will drive to the trailhead, especially if a winter wilderness experience is your goal. Chances are also close to 100 percent that he will do the fly fishing while you slit the pocket bread and stuff it with culinary delights. He will probably carry the tent, knife, compass, stove, and gun while you carry your sleeping bag, clothing, and some food.

The only sensible way to divide roles and gear is by personal preferences. However, in defining preferences, also ask yourself what would happen if you were separated. Who would have the greatest chance of survival? If you can't state a definitive fifty-fifty ratio, then you should do some rearranging. The modification of sex roles is not necessarily a situation in which a man agonizingly gives up his prerogatives. If you volunteer to carry the tent, he will probably respond with indifference or gladly surrender the cumbersome burden. If you ask for the hunting or fishing gear, be prepared for a more violent reaction. Of course, he may respond with delight, but not if your fishing starts to conflict with his own. The obvious solution is to purchase your own gear. If the fly tackle is community property, then insist on equal time. Perhaps you hate fishing or don't like to see the critters die. In this case use barbless hooks and throw the fish back in. Maybe you like to read or take photographs once camp has been set up. Any activities that are mutually beneficial should be mutually shared. This means not only requiring time for yourself, but taking on responsibilities and burdens not usually assigned to women.

Taking on equal responsibilities is a painless way of asserting yourself. Many men are justifiably angry at what they view as a grasping for rights and privileges without a concurrent assumption of responsibility. The more responsibility you take, the better your bargaining position. This means taking part in planning and executing the trip. Take the initiative. Get the maps. Set the date. Watch the weather forecasts. Make sure all of the gear is available and in operating condition. Do at least 50 percent of the driving. Get the stove going or build the fire. Set up the tent. In the midst of all this, you're probably wondering what he will do. Hopefully, 50 percent of the cooking and water fetching, along with washing dishes, clothing, and gathering firewood, and taking care of children.

Personal preferences do emerge, but only through experimenting with all of the available options. Mixing jobs gives each person the opportunity to find out what she or he likes best. Other jobs, such as digging a latrine or changing diapers, are onerous no matter who does them. These should be shared and rotated.

Outings with mixed groups may intensify role expectations. She's with Jim. Her legs are prettier. He's faster. She's overbearing. He's macho. She's an earth mother. And so on.

Traveling in mixed groups for any period of time can prove to be very revealing even if you know your partners well. You'll get to know them a whole lot better before the trip is finished. Chances are very good that even if you have some conflicts on the trail, you will come out of it with a lifelong friendship since you've shared intimacies (and probably some hardships) that even the closest of friends never share in civilization. You may end up disliking a casual acquaintance because you won't be able to escape from contact with him or her. Such are the risks of wilderness adventures, which are never ordinary, either physically or psychologically.

Machismo is a word bantered around a lot. It is a Spanish word meaning strong or assertive masculinity. Many men and women take pride in the macho man, but on the trail he is a liability. A strutting peacock is harmless on the dance floor, but something else again when he wants to cross a steep snow slope without ice axs. While in the field it's often difficult to tell the difference between machismo and reasonable risks. In retrospect, after you're back home, you may shake your head in wonder at why you allowed someone to talk you into crossing a dangerously flooded stream without roping up.

Among ways of determining the difference between reasonable risks and machismo is answering the following questions: (1) What are the objective dangers of the undertaking? (2) Are there reasonable alternatives? (3) Is the person suggesting the risk the type who would try to prove something even if it endangers others? (4) Is the person someone who is experienced enough to know the difference? (5) Are you being pushed into something that is beyond your skill level? (6) Is the benefit worth the potential cost? (7) What are your chances of success?

If you feel uneasy about a situation, follow your instincts. Don't do it. If you are experienced enough to know that you are taking a big chance and decide to do it anyway, that's okay, as long as you're the one who has made the decision.

Little risks are something else again. If it's a nice spring day and you encounter a slippery log you must cross to get over a stream, work up your courage and do it. Even if you slip into the stream, the consequences will probably be minimal. If the log is spiked with sharp points where the branches have broken off, a fall is something else again. Weigh the difference between the chances of major injury versus minor mishaps.

If someone else wants to take what you've determined to be an unreasonable risk, flatly refuse to do it and state your reasons why. Point out that there is a thin line between courage and stupidity, and that you think the line has been crossed. Sit-down strikes or hiding someone's shoelaces, rope, or ice ax will work if you're pressed into a desperate situation. By all means don't cry. Just restate your case until you've worn down the offending party. Of course, all this is much, much easier said than done. Just don't be intimidated into doing something unreasonably dangerous, or inflict this kind of aggression on someone with less experience or more cautious inclinations than your own.

The major difference between hiking with competent men and hiking with competent women in the wilderness is in the arena of competition. Many men, much more so than most women, have a need for competition. Who can get to the top first? Who got their fire built first? Who gets to determine where the campsite should be? Who can go the longest without water?

Too much competition is an insane way to enjoy the wilderness. You really should find out how the men you will be traveling with feel about competition. This goes for some groups of women too, though to a much lesser extent. As they are planning the trip with you, watch for rivalries and one-upsmanship comments. Watch out for groups that tell you that you are the "Queen Bee," the only woman they would consider taking because you can out-perform your gender any day. That's a sure indication that if you fail anywhere, anywhere at all, you will be in disgrace the rest of the trip. The pressure to not fail, not show emotions, perform better than everyone else, prove yourself every minute, can destroy the pleasure of the trip quickly.

Perhaps you are the competitive one. In that case, seek out your own kind and be sure that new members are aware of your group's aggressive attitude.

On the other hand, many men are a pleasure to be with in the wilderness and are able to treat you as an individual with strengths and weaknesses, just as they have. A man who allows himself to show vulnerability or one who has developed empathy is usually a good companion. Men who have hobbies such as wildflowers, mushrooms, photography, geology, or birding are usually more sensitive types. These are more able to accept and feel the world around them on equal terms.

"Are you feminine?" the women surveyed were asked; then, "Do men think you are feminine?" Finally, they were asked if they defined themselves as feminists.

Most of the women said they were feminine. A small minority weren't sure. None said that they were not feminine. These women were all active in the outdoors either professionally or as recreation. When they doubted their femininity it was because men had told them either verbally or by attitude that they weren't. Many said the question had caused great pause for discussion and thought. As one woman said, "When we discussed it [the women in the same city outing program], the more we came to realize that we defined feminine according to men's terms." The same response came from a group of Girl Scouts on a camping trip.

The uncertainty about the definition of feminine and the validity of traditional assumptions showed up most on the second question. Here women were split about fifty-fifty over whether or not men thought they were feminine. Here the maybes almost equaled those who answered yes. Some who were sure that men thought they were feminine said that it was because they were physically attractive to men. "I have long legs and breasts," said one. "I know they think I'm feminine because they want to get into bed with me," said another. "I'm working on it," said another, then revised her answer six months later and decided that femininity isn't something you work on. "It is simply a state of being female," she concluded.

Being feminine is not merely a state of being or physical attractiveness. It is not role playing. It is expressing the qualities of our sex which are positive and it should be encouraged. It includes nurturing, compassion, gentleness, and above all the desire to sustain life. It borders on altruism and can be fierce. Femininity is not passive, masochistic, weak, trivial, or illogical.

The Papoose: Babies and Children

Unless you are already an experienced outdoorswoman who is quite comfortable in the wilderness, it is not advisable to bring along babies or very young children.

Once a baby has enough strength to lift its head, flop over, and crawl, it can be taken with you into the wilds. You will need to be very cautious about sunburn, insect bites, wind, and sudden weather changes as the baby or young child hasn't built up all of its inner immunity to these. Sun that will produce a mild flush on you, or simply deepen your color, can leave a young child burned and miserable.

Baby carriers and packs are the easiest way to carry a baby. Some are adaptable as a front pouch, backpack, or nursing sling. Whoever carries the baby won't have much room for other gear, so will also need a willing companion. You can buy a small fanny pack to carry the baby's gear or attach a stuff bag to your pack.

Disposable diapers need to be burned in a very hot fire. Unburned parts should be carried out. Obviously, diapers should never be rinsed in a stream or water source, and their contents should be buried in the same manner as other human waste.

Karen and Larry Wells, prominent outdoor leaders and enthusiasts from eastern Idaho, have experience in hiking with babies. For very small babies, they have found a front pack works best. When their son, John, was four months old, he fit into the front pack very well. The person carrying the baby can

A babypack adapted to a standard pack frame allows room for other gear.

also wear a backpack. In the winter, the front pack allows the
carrier to share body heat with the baby.

The Wellses have a Gerry Kiddy Pack which works quite
well. Before they were produced, Larry made one from a knap-
sack by cutting holes in the bottom and fixing the shoulder
straps to fasten to a pack frame.

Once they encountered a woman in the Uinta Mountains in
northeastern Utah who had gone a step further by putting a
baby pack on a standard pack frame. This gives better weight
balance and distribution and allows carrying of other equip-

ment. By placing the Gerry Pack in the middle of the standard pack frame, it is easy to use stuff bags for food and gear, fastening them around the baby pack on both sides and bottom. The sleeping bag fits nicely under the baby pack. By the way, the young woman and child were headed into the wilderness to meet her husband and three-year-old son. They had spent ten days in the wilds and decided to stay longer so she had taken the baby and hiked out for more supplies. The woman had covered many miles, including the John Muir Trail, backpacking with a baby.

The Wellses have found it works fine to zip their bags together to sleep the baby, and often a small child, between them.

They use cloth diapers that can be washed by hand, boiled, and hung to dry, saving the disposable diapers for times they think a bowel movement is due. This helps cuts down on bulk and weight.

If the baby is not being breast fed, a powdered formula is used. Breast feeding is most convenient when in the wilds, but a bottle and formula or milk are good to have along in an emergency.

Mosquito netting should be taken, especially for sleeping, since there is no way too keep small children from rubbing insect repellent into their eyes.

The baby must have a hat or some protection from the sun. In addition, small children, up to the age of two, are unable to regulate their body temperature. If it is hot, they must be kept cool by outside sources. If it is cool, they must be warmed by outside sources. Clothing will not take care of it.

The couple took John (then fourteen months old) cross-country skiing when it was a sunny 10 degrees. He was bundled up in several loose layers of wool until he couldn't move. The parents were plenty warm, but after an hour John began to complain. Upon checking, the found his feet and hands were like ice.

They advise taking extra shoes, changes of socks, and clothing since children will always find the nearest mud or water. They have also found that shopping for children's wilderness clothing is best done at thrift stores, since baby clothes for camping are next to impossible to find anywhere else and if available are very expensive.

"Camping with young children and babies requires both parents to help and share the extra burden," John wrote, "so there will be time for each parent to fish, hike or do whatever they enjoy.

"The extra weight and inconvenience is soon overshadowed while watching the child discover the wonders of nature. The chance to watch their wonderment at birds, insects, fish, frogs, flowers and all of God's creation builds a special bond. Even now, when some of the children are busy teenagers with little time for wilderness outings, we still find a common bond and joy in sharing the wilderness experience."

Women who have hiked with babies suggest that you keep trips and mileage short. The extra weight and caring for the child demands that both parents be in good physical condition.

Karen Wells says that the weight of her fourteen-month-old child and her pregnancy weight during a trip into the Salmon River Breaks Primitive Area, combined with the weight of her pack, caused her ankles to collapse. Other members of the party helped carry the baby and some of her gear.

Children between the ages of two and six are heavy to carry and don't have the stamina to walk. Let them hike for awhile, then carry them again. Eventually, they will hike most of the way. During these tender growing years, the youngsters can take short day hikes to build up their strength and aptitude. Young children have a lot of energy for short periods of time, then conk out. At age six children will start hiking longer distances, and they are ready to carry a pack. Day packs, fanny packs, and even children's backpacks can be purchased at most sporting goods stores. An old army surplus bag can serve its purpose here too. Start out easily with lightweight personal items like a treasured but not delicate toy, clothing, toothbrush, cup, and snacks. Eventually, add a sleeping bag and some food. A child won't be able to carry its own complete equipment until it has become a good hiker—can hike the entire distance, no longer complains, and looks forward to trips.

If the child has not been introduced to the wilderness in early years, motivation may be your most difficult task. A child often does not understand the purpose of leaving the security of home, television, and friends for a tiring walk "with nothing to do."

This attitude will probably be less true for boys than for girls. Boys usually associate outdoors trips with being masculine. They think they offer a chance to be with and like their father. Outdoor role models are abundant for boys, while for girls they are rare.

As a mother who wishes to motivate a daughter, you will probably run into problems not of your own doing. Imagine the chagrin of an outdoorswoman should her daughter refuse to have anything to do with knives or canteens because they are boys' toys, or, once she's trekked in a few miles, only wants to play house in the tent or mimic television coffee-making commercials. The mother will have to try to provide a role identity which in many ways is out of step with popular culture. Rather than chiding the girl for accepting traditional models, expand her options by example.

If your family has assumed since the child's birth that everyone will backpack, motivation will be easier. When Karen Wells made her son a backpack, he was very excited and talked in a constant, unintelligible babble, pointing at it. When she would try to put it away, John would scream and cry. As soon as she would put him in the pack, he was once again quiet and cherubic. There will be no trouble motivating John.

The Wellses say that keeping young children occupied is not that difficult. Dr. Jo Ellen Force, a professor of forestry at the University of Idaho, agrees. She always asked some neighbor's children to join hers. Seeing other children their own age hiking along cheerfully egged on the children who were not so excited by the prospect. Together the children could talk about their favorite television shows and entertain each other by the hour. They especially enjoy playing in streams, overturning rocks, building dams, and exploring, says Dr. Force. You just have to be sure that the stream isn't too deep. They'll be occupied for hours and will most likely groan when it's time to leave.

Backpacking trips with children should be short—one-half day of walking at the maximum—so that the children can explore and enjoy themselves the rest of the day. The one-half day of walking can be spread out so that most hiking is done in the cooler mornings and late afternoons.

Teach your child as early as possible what to do if lost. Larry Wells says that one of their daughters became lost but remembered to follow the stream and eventually found her way home. Giving the child a whistle and attiring the youngster in bright clothing will also aid in finding a lost child.

Other survival skills, such as fire building, should be taught as early as possible. The child can participate at a very early age by helping to collect wood. Larry says his children were taught as much as possible and as early as possible so that they could survive in case something happened to the parents.

For hiking shoes for the younger children, Karen makes moccasins or hard-soled socks (Norwegian style) stuffed with a lot of inner socks.

Never borrow boots for your older children. Take care of their feet. If their feet hurt, they will hate hiking. The wrong shoes could cause permanent damage in their foot's growth. Tennis shoes are preferable to borrowed boots. If your child is growing too fast, you may want to buy the boots too large. The oversize can be remedied by wearing several layers of socks or a thick booty inside. Underlayering is not recommended for adults who have a permanent boot size. But, for the sake of economy, for children better a big boot than a little one. Girls are especially awkward to buy boots for. Although current fashions have allowed for boot-like, sturdy shoes to wear with jeans, the current stress is on sandals, flats, tennis shoes, high heels, or non-ankle-supported walking shoes. Buying boots for your girl is a difficult question to answer; should you invest in a pair of boots that will only be worn for one or two summer hikes? Unlike boys, she won't be wearing them to school if she wants to be fashionable. Desert boots are better than tennis shoes and tennis shoes are better than flats.

If you don't buy or adjust for your children the right-size packs and right-size footwear and all the necessary equipment to keep warm that you have, don't expect them to enjoy the outing. Children can get blisters, freeze at night, and have a pack rub them wrong just as you can. You can buy children's equipment at sporting goods sales, secondhand stores, army surplus stores, or garage sales fairly cheaply. Karen Wells buys cheaply a lot a sweaters and pants for her youngest children that people washed in hot water and shrank.

Borrowing and exchanges among neighbors and friends is another possibility. Small women often wear the same sizes as large children, and you might be able to borrow a backpack or other item.

The teens are the most difficult years for the average female in the United States. Caught in the limbo between childhood and adulthood, her self esteem and confidence are not stable. Peer pressure is so strong that not having the right-shaped hip pockets on her pants can make a teenager an outcast—trivial and superficial to be sure, but not her fault. Wilderness camping for girls of this age group is often not the "in" thing. Unless a girl is very independent, rock concerts, hair, makeup application, clothes, boys, and popularity may be her predominant preoccupations.

In the last few years, backpacking and outdoors sports have become much more popular among teenage girls, as has physical fitness. Today most winners of beauty pageants such as Miss USA and Miss America are athletes or at least physically fit. Miss USA 1980 was a weight lifter and runner. Teenage girls, such as Becky Langford of Denver, have begun to grab headlines with their mountaineering accomplishments. The popularity of such endeavors varies throughout the country, but a glance at popular magazines such as Seventeen shows a heavy emphasis on outdoors recreation and some inclination towards the backcountry.

The giant roadblock in this trend is the girl's overriding concern with being attractive to boys and having a lot of friends. Anything that marks her as different or unusual is avoided. The solution is to present backcountry outings as something she can share with her friends. Invite her to invite them.

One way to wean girls into enjoying the outdoors is to give them a half-experience. Take them on a short hike with good food on the menu and social activities planned for the trail's end. Hike them out before dark. Several such adventures makes them more willing to hike further and try and overnighter.

Place some of the responsibility of the hike upon the girls. Let them help you plan the menus, buy the food, practice first aid, build fires, and pack their packs. If you take complete charge, they will feel like the wilderness is an enemy and you are their protector. You will be very tired protecting them all day.

A hike with any group of novices will require diplomacy and kindness. Stragglers should never be isolated or ridiculed. As Carol Alice Liska, a woman who held the summit record for U.S. women mountaineers until 1977 by reaching the summit of Noshaq (24,580 feet), says, "No one should be stuck with being the last on the trail. It's demoralizing. Faster and stronger members of the party should extend the courtesy and empathy to novices to help and encourage them along."

Again, encouragement rather than browbeating is the best approach. Two miles may seem a minor feat to you, but to the beginner, it may be a minimarathon. If you overextend them, this may be the last trip they will ever want to take.

Dogs

You will have to use your judgment on when and where you take a dog. In National Parks, it's illegal. In bear country, it's dangerous. In any country where there's wildlife, a dog is likely to chase the deer or elk unless you've trained him otherwise. Some people insist that a dog should not be taken into the backcountry. Generally, these are not people who own or love dogs. We think a woman, especially one who travels alone, will find a dog an asset since he will notify her of intruders. If he's a big German Sheperd or Doberman, he can help ward off unwelcome human aggressors. Your dog is affected by the long miles, and heat and cold too. In hot places, carry enough water for your dog. Dogs can die of heat exhaustion. In cold places, if your dog is used to house temperatures, you will need to take a blanket or wrap for him at night. You can wrap him in your jacket if you don't mind the smell. Just as you wouldn't expect your grandmother to hike long miles after being indoors all winter, don't expect an older dog to perform the same as in earlier times.

8

Organized Outings

Wilderness lovers are notoriously independent, feisty, difficult, and opinionated. Why then do they go on organized trips?

Those who are new to backcountry activities prefer to join organized trips to learn, and to enjoy their adventures without suffering over much from ignorant mistakes. Organized group outings also give an added safety factor. Fall and break a leg all alone, and chances are slender of anyone finding you in time to call a helicopter. Difficult ventures such as white water kayaking, rock climbing, and cross-country skiing, are risky enough that they should rarely, if ever, be attempted alone. If you want to risk your neck and get into trouble and face the consequences, that's your affair. If you take such risks and expect the Search and Rescue to put its employees' lives on the line to haul you back out, it ceases to be your own business.

The National Park Service frowns on solo outings because it doesn't have the time, money, or personnel to keep track of inexperienced lone travelers. The park service has also been

Credit for much of the information in this chapter goes to Slim Woodruff. The authors thank her for her assistance with the writing.

the victim of numerous suits in which a tourist took an obvious risk yet blamed the park service for the outcome. The legal thinking in Europe is much different on this point. There the state is not responsible for what the public takes on itself. If you've wondered why park service employees act like cops, much of it is because of an irresponsible, ignorant public that expects the wilds to be as easy to maneuver as a shopping mall.

Although the solo experience is important, many people don't have as good a time alone as with convivial companions. Unless one has a bevy of friends at the same skill level, who are interested in the same places and have the same days off from work, it is difficult to arrange for a group trip.

Many people enjoy club organized outings. It's a way to meet others. Outdoors-type people are always on the lookout for someone to arrange trips with. Since many of the dedicated are the footloose and fancy free who are found one week in Oregon, the next in Colorado, and the next in southern Utah, they are hard to track down for a weekend trip. Until such time as they manage to be in the same place, it is easier to go on a club trip and let someone else do the organizing.

Club Outings

Most organized trips are run by local outing and hiking clubs. To find one, try a mountaineering store, university outdoor program, or environmental organization. The casual trip, where everyone more or less gets together and wanders up the trail, is better for the more experienced. If you want to learn something about hiking, rafting, or climbing, you had best go on a trip with a strong leader. In a leaderless group you are likely to be found wandering at the tail end, looking confused, while everyone else is going about their own business and ignoring you. That's why they came on the trip. And that's why they support a club which operates in this manner.

Many outing clubs, national and local Sierra Club trips, city parks and recreation programs, American Youth Hostels, and the YW/YMCA have a specific outing leader. Fees, to cover the costs of the leader, are often levied. Depending on the organization, these leaders have to meet certain requirements. The

Phoenix Sierra Club, for example, requires trip leaders to have Advanced First Aid and to attend leadership workshops. On the other hand, the Northern Arizona University Hiking Club would allow absolutely anyone to lead a trip so long as she had access to a car and knew about where the trailhead was. At Idaho State University many trips are organized by someone simply posting a sign-up sheet. It may sound callous to let new people fumble about on their own, but responsibility cuts in on your own time to enjoy the outing. Not a lot of people are willing to assume it if not being paid.

An assigned leader who is conscientious will make sure the people in the front of the line know the trail, the people in the back of the line stay there so no one strays off, checks to be sure everyone has water and lunch, and altogether acts as a tactful babysitter. The effort is not always appreciated. On one hiking trip with no assigned leader, a veteran tried to help out a novice who was having some trouble. She suggested some ways to cut down the weight of the pack and checked around to be sure the campsite would be left clean while the novice was throwing things away. In return for her pains, the experienced woman was snarled at and told she acted like a sergeant in boot camp. Judging that her aid was not wanted, she donned her pack, hiked out of sight, and sat on a high rock watching the novice get hopelessly lost. Eventually, she did relent and tell the other woman where the trail was.

Usually, the only time a leader doesn't emerge within a group is when good friends get together. In this situation, if skills are equal, no one is willing to accept orders from anyone else. With strangers, a lot of problems can be avoided by assigning a trip leader.

If hiking with a group of friends or a club, it sometimes helps to make a list of things you really wish to accomplish and those which you're willing to bend on. This gives you a bargaining stance, rather than complaining every time the schedule is changed or something is taken off the itinerary.

When someone organizes a trip for friends or a club, she does a lot of logistics work. She plans the caches, if on an extended trip or where there's little water; buys the food for group use, packages it, arranges for drop-offs at the roadhead, pick-ups, shuttles, and pools. For out-of-town friends, she arranges places to stay. She writes for the permits, collects the maps, plans the routes, and sometimes hands out equipment lists. No wonder people go on organized trips and let someone else do all that work for them!

While most local club trips are not so finely crafted, they do at least plan the route and arrange for transportation to be shared. If you are a beginner, you can ask for advice, and will usually receive all you can handle. Aside from being independent, feisty, difficult and opinionated, outdoors people love to pontificate on their theory of hiking, river running, rock climbing, or skiing. This is a great help if you want to learn or just pick up some new pointers and opinions on the skill.

Guides and Outfitters

Club outings are fairly hit and miss. It is purely luck to find a leader who enjoys being with people as opposed to simply showing off: a leader who thinks of the small comforts, like making sure everyone has a full water bottle rather than letting them learn by experiencing a dry mouth at lunch; a leader who will show you where you are on the map and point out landmarks instead of shuffling on through, nose in the air, while you try to figure out what you are looking at. They are, in a word, unsung. They do it out of the goodness of their hearts. Others are so mean as to hike off and let someone get lost just because they argued, complained, or moved too slowly.

So what about hiring a professional guide or outfitter? On a professional trip the leader is there specifically to watch over you, teach you, entertain you, and see to it that you have a good time. This is what they're paid for. It is what they have chosen to do. You can ask all the dumb questions you like and they will usually answer them with a smile.

Some trips are almost always led by an outfitter, such as in whitewater rafting. Few of us have the capital to buy the rafts and gear, or the time to become expert enough to run a bad river.

Horsepack trips are also more often reserved for those with the know-how, experience, and most of all, the horses. Rock and ice-climbing schools are highly recommended over taking off on your own with a piece of clothesline to teach yourself. Expeditions, such as Mt. Denali in Alaska or a winter ascent of Mt. Whitney in California, are best not attempted by the casual backpacker who would like to get in a bit of snow camping. If you lack patient and loving friends who are skilled and willing to teach you what they know, an outfitter may be your best bet.

Choose your outfitter according to what you want out of the experience. Donna Jean Cole, who owns and operates the Wilderness Experience Backpacking School in Remsen, New York, advises to ask specifically for the philosophy of the organization. If you're looking for a week-long trip without the hassles of buying the food, equipment, and other items, and don't care much about learning the subtle differences between a Kelty packframe and a Camp Trails, all you need do is find someone who knows the country and is a good cook. If you want to learn enough skills to take off on your own, you need an organization that defines itself as a school rather than as an outfitter.

Send for several brochures. Look through outdoor magazines for their addresses. Especially check the small print in the classified ads. Obviously, outfitters and schools put their best foot forward in their literature, but you can get an idea of what's going on. Some outfitters don't expect you to do any more hiking than from the car to the demarcation point. Some jeep or fly clients into areas; some use horses; some do only backpacking or have the packstring carry the gear while you walk. One outfit runs week-long trips into the high Rockies with gourmet food and a live band—all packed in on horses.

Some schools run the hairy, scare-the-student-into-proficiency programs where you claw your way up and down sheer rocks and spend nights out on solo with only yourself and the food you can find with your grubby little hands. The brochures will help you narrow down the type of outfitter or school you're looking for.

Write or call those you are considering. Are any of the trips led by women, or is the only female employee the cook? If so, you might want to consider the attitude the organization will have toward you as a woman.

How long has the company been in business? Do they have

preplanned trips or do they arrange it all around you and your group? Ask how long the trips are, and how arduous the journey. If you want to top peaks, ask if they do that. If you want to take pictures of flowers, find out when they are at their peak.

What requirements do they have for guides? Are they trained in first aid? Do they know natural history? Some people are frustrated if they can't be told the names of 90 percent of the plants they see. Are the areas scouted first? River guides are usually closely monitored by a government agency. They have to be competent to keep their licenses. Not only do they know the river, often acquiring those permits requires a college degree in recreation, archaeology, counseling, or something that might be of value when dealing with clients.

What does an outfitter give you for your money? The less work you have to do and the more elaborate or dangerous the trip, the more it costs. Some provide only the food and you bring your own gear. Many have some kind of rental service at additional cost. Some supply everything but your clothing. Some of the latter will give a discount if you do bring your own gear.

Some, particularly survival, stress, and challenge schools, tell you as little as possible about what to bring and what to expect. These want you to learn by making your own mistakes. Others will supply you with a detailed list of supplies to bring, reading lists for background of the area and sport, and will answer your questions in detail. Some include personal questionnaires asking about physical fitness, interests, and food preferences. In the stress-challenge program for which one woman worked, the students completed a questionnaire on why they wanted to participate, what they wanted to learn, and what they expected from the experience.

Donna Jean Cole requires a full-day session of orientation before the trip is made. However, Donna is a teacher, not an outfitter.

Word of mouth information can be the most valuable. Ask friends what they thought of their guides. Ask the outfitter or school for references and follow up on these.

Depending on the trip, you can expect to be directed to meet at some centrally located town with an airport whence the trip will originate. Some outfitters, notably river runners, will throw your gear into the boat, sit you down, and take off with nary a word but to hold on. The stress-challenge programs one woman worked for drove the novices into the woods, went through their packs and threw out the things they didn't need, then abandoned them in the dark to find their way to the campsite—marked by a large fire. This was called dynamic introduction. It tended to scare a number of them thoroughly.

As a backpack guide, Slim Woodruff meets the people the day before the hike and goes through their gear. "If they are using our equipment, I familiarize them with it and show them how to pack it. If they bring their own, I check it to be sure it will withstand harsh weather, will be comfortable, and keep them safe." She still shudders to think of the man who insisted on bringing his own tent. She was not real sure of its quality, but was assured that he'd used it before and loved it. She let it pass. It turned out to be a shelter tent, uncoated nylon, not waterproofed, and his group was completely soaked the first night out. "Now I unroll every piece of equipment and no longer take a client's word for anything. If I don't pass an item, I replace it with good rental gear."

If a guide or instructor does check your gear, and she should, is it explained why or why not you should pack or leave something? Do they casually throw out your three pairs of jeans, or do they stop to explain that when backpacking only take one pair to save on weight? Many women want to bring a change of fresh clothing for each day. But when Slim explains that they will be donning clean clothing over a far from clean body, they usually see the point.

Please listen to your guide. You are paying for the help. Do not, if advised to take a down parka, leave it behind on the theory that since it is almost 90 degrees down in the valley, it can't possibly be that cold in the mountains. Guides tend to get upset if someone leaves gear behind and then tries to borrow theirs. Most guides are all for clients cutting down on weight, but not if they depend on the use of the guide's day pack, foam pad, cup and spoon, and paperback book.

Some schools will issue a student a bag of raw materials such as cornmeal, sugar, flour, and salt, and allow her to make her own meals. Most outfitters, on the other hand, pack a complete repertory of freeze-dried and fresh foods—from blueberry pancakes with bacon to beef chop suey decked with almonds on to fresh-baked gingerbread.

On trips specifically for those who want to learn outdoors skills, the guide will take extra time to lecture on equipment, techniques, and how and what to do at every turn. On other trips, many aren't so loquacious for fear of being a bore. If the guide isn't talking, it may be because she figures you already know it. If you want to learn, ask. Most people are in love with the sound of their own voices, and will talk your ear off if they know you want to listen. Some guides have been through this routine a dozen times and tend to forget if they have already mentioned the advantages of white gas over butane stoves to this particular group.

If under your own power as opposed to on horseback or rafting, the venture should be paced so that you do not have to kill yourself getting to the destination. When backpacking, some guides take two days to climb into a high mountain basin, then set up a base camp to day-hike from. The first day is the hardest. In high country, you have to allow some time to acclimatize. On any hike, it seems to take one or two days for your body to adjust somewhat to carrying the pack. In our experience, things get much better by the third day.

What if the rest of the group is faster or slower than you, and you don't want to annoy or be annoyed? Sometimes everyone on the trip is at the same ability level, and that's dandy. You can sally along at your own speed and stay in the group to chat, groan, or mutter to each other. If some members of the group are weaker or stronger, things get more complex. The guide cannot force the slower people to go faster than is comfortable for them, keeping in mind that the group does need to be to camp before dark. But it can be almost as tiring for faster members to move slower than they are used to.

On hikes that Slim leads, she usually lets the faster people go ahead. She tells them where to stop and wait, then she stays with those at the end of the line. If those ahead become confused by the trail, they can always sit down and cool their heels until the rest catch up. She almost always walks at the end of the group. This allows the group to pace itself. "I tend to forget that I can stroll up a mountain all day long without having to stop, but my clients are not in that kind of physical condition," she says. "When I first started guiding, I never quite believed that I wasn't stopping too often, and that the clients weren't getting bored by going too slow. Instead, I was always accused of walking impossibly fast, so I started hiking behind everyone else."

Quite often she times her rest stops. Her long stops are planned ahead of time to take advantage of the end of a switchback, a stream, or just a fantastic view. She also makes sure never to hike more than one-half hour on flat terrain, or fifteen minutes when gaining elevation, without a short breather.

Basically, guides should be more concerned with your having a good time than themselves. There are adjustments to be made. Sometimes the slower people will have to work longer and harder. Sometimes the faster ones will have to settle on not getting as far. Not everyone in the group will want to climb a peak. It may be necessary, if there is just one guide, to drop off some of the group at a lake or meadow halfway up, take the summit, and return to pick up the others.

How about going on an outing with all those strangers? It can be unsettling to be flung into a group of people who have convened from the four corners of the continent. They come from all professions and persuasions, with varying experience in the outdoors, and here you are clustered in intimacy far into the wilderness. You must share the woods for your toilet, and probably a tent to sleep in.

Most people in this situation are on their best behavior. They are dealing with strangers too, and during the first phase of the trip are all trying to be friendly and impress each other with what good sports they are. When they get tired and hungry, or cold and scared, the attitude may slip, but for the most part, they will try to be agreeable.

Second, these people are on vacation. They have made up their minds to enjoy the experience. They may run into setbacks which could spoil a whole day, such as snow in June, washed out trails, or blisters, and take them in stride. They may even consider the hardships an added bit of fillip to the trip.

It doesn't matter how many self-knowledge courses the guide

has taken, how self reliant, or how understanding and empathetic, some people just don't get along. Some people make inappropriate jokes. They are nasty, crude, lazy or spoiled. They act as if they have the IQ and sensitivity of a crowbar. They can spoil everybody's day with little effort. They don't show up on backcountry trips very often, but sometimes they do.

A guide has the right to ask anyone to leave the group if it is felt they are detracting from the experience or may cause danger to themselves and others. However, most guides will avoid this because it means taking the time to escort the culprit back to civilization. As a client, the best solution in dealing with an obnoxious person is to ignore and avoid them. Often, the shunning by other members of the party will bring the offender into line.

Both Slim and Donna Jean comment that as guides and teachers they emphasize to their clients the importance of not destroying the wilds they enter. "In the twelve years I've been backpacking around the Adirondacks," says Donna, "it became apparent that unless people could be educated in the use of the wilderness, the great numbers of them would eventually destroy such areas. Thus WEBS (Wilderness Experience Backpacking School) was born."

"I look at it this way," says Slim, "most of these people would go anyway, one way or another. If they are with me, they are safer and do less damage than they would on their own. I choose to believe that most littering, illegal campfires, water pollution, desecration of historic sites, and mistreatment of wildlife is due to ignorance, not maliciousness. Many people do not realize that a casually tossed pop top can spell death to a fish or animal which eats it; that discarded film negatives from instant cameras can be ingested by a deer with fatal results; or that an innocuous six-pack plastic ring can trap and kill a small animal. From me, and guides like me, clients can learn all these things from the start."

Considering Women

Classes, outings, and organizations that devote themselves either exclusively or primarily to women in the wilderness are merely recognizing a need and a market for women to become a part of the backcountry experience on their own. The arrival of such organizations and offerings can be traced only a few years back to the late 1970s.

"Personally, I would have to say that I think there's been a definite increase in the number of women interested in backpacking, mountaineering, ski touring, et cetera, in recent years," says Howie Wolke, co-owner of Wild Horizons Expeditions in Jackson, Wyoming and Wyoming representative of Friends of the Earth. "However, certain of the 'hard core' activities such as multi-day winter trips, long solo backpacking and so forth, still seem to be predominantly male."

Correspondingly, most of the outfitters and schools contacted noted an increase in the number of women participants. The smallest, true to Howie's observation, was in long winter expeditions such as those organized by Lynx Track Winter Travel in Excelsior, Minnesota. Here, according to Lynx staffer Duncan Storlie, there has been a very small increase, although he notes that the school has done trips exclusively for women.

The 'hard core' activities require skills acquired in less demanding outings. As the number of women increases in the latter, so will it in the former.

Among the many hopeful trends is the women's mountaineering course offered by the National Outdoor Leadership School. The course has been a considerable success, according to John Sullivan, director of development and public affairs for NOLS. Its purpose is to encourage women who would prefer to learn their skills from other women, and in the company of other women, to participate in NOLS training.

Similarly, the wilderness studies program at the University of California extension in Santa Cruz offers an occasional basic backpacking course for women to attract them into the larger program. While these courses seem to be based on the concept of remedial training, there is validity to the concept since many women want and need such training, much as some college freshmen need courses in remedial English before they can go on to the general college curriculum.

Others, such as trips and classes offered by Osprey River

Trips, Inc., seem to be based more on the affirmation and support of women and the concept of a unique female approach to nature.

Osprey's programs include a Women's Whitewater School, Women's Dream Workshop, and Women in the Outdoors. "Our all-women trips attracted women from all over the nation, ranging in ages from eighteen to fifty-six," commented Anna M. Alden, president of Osprey. "Women responded with great excitement, courage, and interest in the river and its environment. The support and camaraderie which grew between women in the course of the trips was a constant source of personal and professional satisfaction for myself and the other women with whom I work."

Among national volunteer organizations that exist specifically for women, not as an extension of an organization's other activities, are Women in the Wilderness; Camping Women; and American Women's Himalayan Expeditions, organized in tandem with the American Alpine Club.

Women in the Wilderness started in 1976 and maintains a national network of contacts, trips, classes, and casual outings. Male members are accepted if their attitudes are compatible with the organization vs. stating the "why" of the organization, WW says, "Outdoor adventuring has become a predominant ly male domain. As a result, women often depend on men with more skills to take fuller responsibility and to provide learning opportunities on wilderness trips. To move toward equality and independence in outdoor adventures, we believe there is value for women to participate in adventures with other women. This furnishes us with opportunities to gain new skills, be fully responsible, and see one another in the role of competent and independent adventurers."

WW publishes a quarterly journal which includes wilderness information, outing schedules, regional contacts, philosophy and theory, and artwork. In addition, it publishes a monthly newsletter titled, *Good News: Outdoor Job Information for Women.*

Samples of WW's outing directory are plant identification and botanical technique, mother-daughter trips, Vermont bicycle touring, nordic skiing, backpacking, canoeing, and many like-minded nonprofit and profit schools, outfitters, and groups and clubs.

Like WW, Camping Women offers trips at cost and is staffed by volunteers.

Camping Women publishes a monthly newspaper which also lists outings, chapter contacts, and information about outdoors skills. Although CW's emphasis is principally on self-propelled recreation, it does offer information for those who seek the backcountry experience in Winnebagos.

The American Women's Himalayan Expeditions is the group responsible for putting the first all-woman United States expedition atop any of the world's mountains above 26,000 feet. Of necessity, it is not the populist type of organization such as Women in the Wilderness and Camping Women. It appears to operate on the same premise as the American Alpine Club, which is by invitation. Like WW and CW, it is a child of the late 1970s. Some of AWHE's principal functions are to raise money for its expeditions and to train women in the skills needed to do this type of demanding mountaineering.

Numerous other regional and state organizations are either specifically organized for women or take women into consideration by offering trips for them. As national networks, Women in the Wilderness and Camping Women can help you find those in your area.

Schools, Outfitters, and Groups Offering Outings for Women

(Most outfitters will schedule an all-woman's trip if a client can organize the members for the outing. Outfitters included in this listing are those who regularly schedule such outings or have in the past.)

1. American Women's Himalayan Expeditions
   c/o The American Alpine Club
   113 East 90th Street
   New York, New York 10028

2. Artemis Tours
   Box 5749
   Austin, Texas 78763

3. Blackberry Creek Camp
   Box 28
   Pulga, California 95965

4. Camping Women
   2720 Armstrong Drive
   Sacramento, California 95825

5. Encounter Four
   Butler County Community College
   Butler, Pennsylvania 16001

6. Good Travel Tours, Pacific Encounters
   5332 College Avenue
   Oakland, California 94618

7. The Infinite Odyssey
   25 Huntington Avenue, Suite 324
   Boston, Massachusetts 02155

8. Keep Listening
   Box 446
   Sandy, Oregon 97055

9. Lynx Track Winter Travel
   5375 Eureka Road
   Excelsior, Minnesota 55331

10. National Outdoor Leadership School
    Department G
    Box AA
    Lander, Wyoming 82520

11. Nature Explorations
    1176 Emerson Street
    Palo Alto, California 94301

12. Oberlin College Wilderness Program
    Box 204
    Cleveland, Ohio 44106

13. Osprey River Trips
    6109 Fish Hatchery Road
    Grants Pass, Oregon 97526

14. The Outdoor Woman's School
    25190 Cedar Street
    Berkeley, California 94708

15. Outdoors Unlimited
    Recreation Dept. 783
    Guy Millberry Union #238
    University of Calif. at S.F.
    San Francisco, California 94143

16. Outward Bound, Colorado
    945 Pennsylvania Street
    Denver, Colorado 80203

17. Outward Bound, Dartmouth Center
    Box 50
    Hanover, New Hampshire 03755

18. Outward Bound, Hurricane Island
    Box 429
    Rockland, Maine 04841

19. Outward Bound, Minnesota
    308 Walker Avenue, South
    Wayzata, Minnesota 55391

20. Outward Bound, North Carolina
    Box 817
    Morganton, North Carolina 28655

21. Outward Bound, Northwest
    0110 S.W. Bancroft Street
    Portland, Oregon 97201

22. Outward Bound, Southwest
    Box 2840
    Santa Fe, New Mexico 87501

23. Palisades School of Mountaineering
    Box 694
    Bishop, California 93514

24. Sierra Kayak School
    Box 682
    Lotus, California 95651

25. Trailhead Ventures
    Box CC
    Buena Vista, Colorado 81211

26. Underway
    Touch of Nature Environmental Center
    Southern Illinois University
    Carbondale, Illinois 62901

27. Washington Women Outdoors
    Garrett Park, Maryland 20766

28. White Pine Touring Center
    Box 417
    Park City, Utah 84060

29. Wilderness Experience Backpacking School
    R.D. No. 2
    Remsen, New York 13438

30. Wilderness Learning Institute
    2445 Park Avenue South
    Minneapolis, Minnesota 55404

31. Wilderness Studies
    University of California Extension
    Santa Cruz, California 95064

32. Wilderness Trips
    Box 207
    Lake Lenore, Saskatchewan, SOK 2J0

33. Wind Over Mountain
    Box 2724
    Evergreen, Colorado 80439

34. Wolfcreek Wilderness School
    Box 596
    Blairsville, Georgia 30512

35. Woman's Way Adventures
    Box 1182
    Tahoe City, California 95730

36. Women in the Wilderness
    474 Boston Avenue
    Medford, Massachusetts 02155

37. Women Outdoors
    474 Boston Avenue
    Medford, Massachusetts 02155

38. Woodswomen
    3716 4th Avenue, South
    Minneapolis, Minnesota 55409

Getting Over the Border

Backcountry travel in a foreign country should be approached cautiously and with methodical planning and investigation. The less the country's culture resembles our own, the more radical will be the difference in attitudes towards women. Attitudes toward women, in general, worldwide are not as advanced as they are in the United States. The less westernized the country, the more likely the restrictions.

Most women who have done backcountry expeditions in countries, such as Mexico, Australia, and the Pacific Islands, recommend that such trips be taken with a North American or European guide.

Joyce Lee English, who spent ten weeks in central Mexico on a college biology expedition, doesn't recommend an all-woman group for such a venture. She cites the presence of highwaymen (bandidos), language, and culture as reasons. "It would be very obvious to anyone who saw you, and likely not safe," she says. She further advises to wear a skirt or dress in town at all times even if one wears hiking boots with the dress. "You must respect general customs since not doing so truly offends the natives." She recommends to wear pants only when out of town.

As noted by Arlene Blum, expedition leader, in her book, *Annapurna, A Woman's Place*, tampons were not available in

Nepal. They are often not available in other foreign countries as is true, but less so, of sanitary napkins.

Naomi J. Kahn, vice president of Good Travel Tours, Pacific Encounters, comments that her company did run its first all-female expedition recently. "It worked out very well except in traditional Fijian villages, where the women of the village wanted to confine our group to traditional women's activities, and our group wanted to try everything. We plan to gradually chip away at this attitude, but we know it will take time."

Similarly, Merle Friendenberg, one of the founding partners of Adventure Centers, said that on their trips, particularly through Muslim countries, the traditional attitudes toward women must be carefully taken into account.

Hiking in European countries is very social and controlled. Probably the most obvious differences between them and United States is loss of solitude and the obvious remnants of man.

In England, it is a common practice for the populace to take Sunday hikes into the countryside. Paths through farmer's fields and state-owned forests abound. "Stiles" are provided as a means of crossing barbed wire fences or stone hedges. If you backpack, there are only a few wild forests available. In comparison to North American forests, there is little wild undergrowth. Open fires are allowed but they are built on tins above the ground. Some dead wood is available although coals, such as those used for barbecues are more common. Long pants are accepted for women but short ones are not. There are "rangers" in England who live in small huts on the forests. One woman ranger managed a wild horse herd and dirt road through her section of the forest. There is no concept of wilderness in England, or for that matter, in all of Europe.

In Wales, it is a custom to climb the mountains in large family groups on holidays and weekends. Beautiful hiking sticks are sported by the men. Many families sing together as they hike. The Welsh pride themselves on being a singing nation. Wales is quite beautiful and retains a lot of historical character.

In Scotland, you can go for miles without seeing a hut or farm. But if you walk out upon the bare moors, there are sheep droppings everywhere. It is difficult to find a place to sit without encountering several of these gems. Scotland can be very cold, windy, and harsh for a backcountry expedition.

In Norway where she lives, Norma Jean Sands, American oceanographer and experienced backpacker, reports that backpackers use "warming huts." Pots and pans, utensils, and convenient bunk beds await the hiker. Norma said that the Norwegians are very surprised when she prefers to pitch her tent elsewhere or sleep in her sleeping bag outside under the stars.

In Switzerland, the scenerly is beautiful but solitude is almost nonexistent. Just when you settle down in some sunny vale off the beaten path, the bells of a goatherd can soon be heard tinkling in your vicinity. The herder is not far behind.

The Youth Hostel is a primitive hotel in Europe made to accommodate the backpacker. Most land in Europe belongs to someone or is used for a specific purpose so you can never get away from civilization. These hostels are clean, refurbished homes and castles which provide good, cheap meals and shelters in return for a few cleanup chores from you. Water in streams, lakes, or local fountains is usually polluted in Europe. Water should be bought in bottles or collected from the tap of hostels, good restaurants, and hotels. A woman backpacker will find it difficult to find a bathroom in Europe and will often have to resort to a quick trip behind the nearest bush. Urinals are provided in most major towns for men. Gas stations are not as plentiful in Europe nor are they always outfitted with a bathroom.

If you backpack in Europe, your purpose should be more for an inexpensive means of seeing history and enjoying people. Solitude, contemplation, and a chance to get away from it all, such as you experience in the wilds of North America, are rare in the Europe of today.

A number of trail guidebooks have been written on such countries as Peru and Bolivia, Mexico and Central America, the Canadian Rockies, Nova Scotia, and the Alps.

Without the guidebooks, and even with them in some cases, backcountry travel is going to be more difficult in undeveloped parts of the world. Popular vacation areas such as the Alps have well-developed trail systems and outings organized through the chalets. But other areas mean leaving behind not only one's native tongue and culture, but the wonderful USGS maps.

The U.S. Defense Mapping Agency has maps for most of the world. However, many of these are on a large 1:100,000 scale. In addition, the U.S. Department of Commerce, Division of Tourism, has some aeronautical and nautical maps as well as tourist information which may be useful. Another potential source for maps and general information is the National Geographic Society. Addresses for all of these sources are included at the end of this chapter. Some of these agency maps may be available through a university or big city library, although the collection will probably be erratic at best.

Further information should be obtained from the consulate of the country in question. If you live in a large city such as San Francisco or New York, the consulate office will be listed in the telephone book. Otherwise, consulate addresses can be found in the "Congressional Directory" in the government documents section of a large library in your area.

In addition to foreign countries, Alaskan travel requires special consideration. Backpacking and river running in Alaska are vastly different than they are anywhere in the lower forty-eight states, says Linda Burke, who has done both. Navigation skills are a must, according to every woman surveyed who'd been there.

One cannot move around in Alaska like in the lower forty-eight. First, the ground is covered with tundra and beneath that is permafrost, says Linda. It is very spongy and wet which makes walking difficult and results in millions of mosquitoes. Because of the logistical problems of traveling over land, rivers are used much like roads are used in the lower forty-eight. Because there are much fewer roads, mountains are hard to get to and there are very few hiking trails. There are good trails in limited areas only.

Linda further comments that many Alaskan rivers are flat water by comparison to the whitewater of the Salmon or Colorado Rivers. Although Alaskan rivers such as the Alsek or the Susitna provide some of the biggest whitewater in the world, many others have very little drop. "They originate in very high mountains and most are glacier fed. The glaciers come so far down the mountains, that the actual river has very little drop. Because of this, many are flat, wide, and muddy," she says. However, river running is exciting because most have no roads into them, and once there the person is committed to getting herself out. "There's no rescue service, except what you arrange on your own," she says.

In all situations, foreign countries and Alaska, as well as in the continental United States, pretrip planning should include, if possible, a talk with the locals or people who have been there. "I once went diving off a reef off the Australian coast and found out later that the guy fishing on the beach was fishing for sharks!" says Joyce. "I should have checked ahead of time to see if the water was safe."

Outdoor and Women's Job Newsletters, Listings, and Services

1. Association for Experiential Education
   Box 4265
   Denver, Colorado 80204

2. National Recreation and Park Association
   1601 North Kent Street
   Arlington, Virginia 22209

3. "Good News: Outdoor Job Information for Women"
   Women in the Wilderness
   Fort Mason Bldg. 201
   San Francisco, California 94128

4. "Civil Service Career Opportunities"
   Federal Research Service, Inc.
   Box 1059
   Vienna, Virginia 22180

5. National Directory of Women's Employment Programs
   Wider Opportunities for Women, Inc.
   1649 K Street, N.W.
   Washington, D.C. 20006

6. Office of the Secretary
   Women's Bureau
   U.S. Department of Labor
   Washington, D.C. 20210

7. "Women in Action"
   Federal Women's Program
   Office of Personnel Management
   Washington, D.C. 20415

8. "Job Hunter's Kit"
   American Association of University Women
   Sales Office
   2401 Virginia Avenue, N.W.
   Washington, D.C. 20037

9. Girl Scouts of USA
   830 Third Avenue
   New York, N.Y. 10022

Notes

Chapter One
The Outdoorswoman

1. McGuiness, Diane, "Sex Differences in the Organization of Perception and Cognition," in *Exploring Sex Differences*, edited by Barbara Lloyd and John Archer (Hertfordshire, England: Academic Press, 1976), p. 143.
2. Ibid., p. 136.
3. Ibid., p. 130.
4. Ibid., p. 129.
5. McGrew, W.C., "Aspects of Social Development," in *Ethological Studies of Child Behavior*, edited by N. Blurton-Jones (Cambridge University Press, 1972).
6. Weller, G.M. and Bell, R.Q., "Basal Skin Conductance and the Neonatal State," in *Child Development*, 36 (1965):647–657.
7. Fox, Dr. Edward L., *Sports Physiology* (Columbus, Ohio: W.B. Saunders Co., 1979), p. 104.
8. Nunneley, Sarah A., "Physiological Responses of Women to Thermal Stress: A Review," in *Medicine and Science in Sports 10*, No. 4 (1978), pp. 250–255.
9. Ibid.
10. Ibid.

11. Wells, Christine L., *The Physician and Sports Medicine*, 5, no. 9 *(September 1977)*: pp. 79–90.

12. Ibid.

13. Fox, op. cit., p. 212.

14. Hannon, John P., *Environmental Stress: Individual Human Adaptations* (San Francisco: Academic Press, 1978), pp. 335–349.

15. Hackett, Peter H., and Drummond, Rennie, "Rales, Peripheral Edema, Retinal Hemorrhage and Acute Mountain Sickness." *American Journal of Medicine*, 67 (1979):pp. 214–218.

16. Seghers, Carroll, *The Peak Experience* (New York: Bobbs-Merrill, 1979), p. 32.

17. Lind, A. R. and Petrofsky, J. S., "The Influences of Age, Sex and Body Fat Content on Isometric Strength and Endurance," in *Environmental Stress: Individual Human Adaptations* (New York: Academic Press, 1978).

18. Stewart, George R., *Ordeal by Hunger, The Story of the Donner Party* (Boston: Houghton Mifflin Co., 1960), p. 117.

19. Oakley, Ann., *Sex, Gender and Society* (New York: Harper and Row, 1972), p. 26.

20. Weitz, Shirley, *Sex Roles: Biological, Psychological and Social Foundations* (Oxford: Oxford University Press, 1977), p. 15.

21. Rogers, Lesley, "Male Hormones and Behavior," in *Exploring Sex Differences*, edited by Lloyd, Barbara and Archer, John (New York: Academic Press, 1976), pp. 157–184.

22. Ibid.

23. Weitz, op. cit., p. 15.

24. Ibid.

Chapter Two
Equipment

1. Corry, Patricia, "Letter to the Editor," *Women in the Wilderness Quarterly* June July August 1979, p. 4.

Chapter Three
Physical Fitness

1. Nunneley, Sarah A. "Interview," *The Physician and Sports Medicine*, Vol. 5, no. 9, Sept. 1977.

2. Oakley, Ann, *Sex, Gender and Society* (New York: Harper and Row, 1972), pp. 28–29.

3. Emmerton, Bill, "Bill Emmerton's Book of Running," *Today's Jogger*, 2, no. 11 (July 1979): pp. 34–39.

4. Percy, E.C., "Erogenic Aids in Athletics," *Medicine and Science in Sports*, no. 10, Vol. 4 (Winter 1978): p. 299.

5. Fox, op. cit., p. 211.

6. Brown, C. Harmon and Wilmore, Jack H., "Alterations in Strength, Body Composition and Anthropometric Measurements Consequent to a 10-Week Training Program," *Medicine and Science In Sports*, No. 2 (1974): 133–138.

7. Kaplan, Jannice, *Women and Sports* (New York: Viking Press, 1979), p. 43.

8. Meyers, C. R., "Effects of Two Isometric Routines on Strength, Size and Endurance in Exercised and Nonexercised Arms," *Research Quarterly*, 38 (1967): 430–440.

Chapter Four
Great Expectations

1. Rustrum, Calvin, *The Wilderness Route Finder* (New York: MacMillan Publishing Co., 1967), p. 17.

2. Ibid., p. 3.

3. Stankey, George H., "Visitor Perception of Wilderness Recreation Carrying Capacity," U.S. Department of Agriculture, Forest Service Resource Papers, INT–142, p. 61.

Chapter Five
Fail Safe for the Better Half

1. McGrath, E. and Phillips, B.J., "Women and Sports," *Time*, 26 June 1978, p. 54–60.

2. "Leg Pains in Runners: A Round Table," *The Physician and Sports Medicine*, 5, no. 9 (September 1977): pp. 42–53.

3. Ibid.

4. Wilkerson, James A., *Medicine for Mountaineering* (Seattle, Washington: The Mountaineers, 1975), pp. 101–102.

5. Darden, Ellington, *Especially for Women* (New York: Leisure Books), pp. 56–64.

6. Lind, A.R., and Petrofsky, J.S., "The Influence of Age, Sex, and Body Fat Content on Isometric Strength and Endurance," *Environmental Stress: Individual Human Adaptation* (New York: Academic Press, 1978).

7. Allsen, P.E.; Parsons, P.; Bryce, G.R., "The Effect of Menses on Maximal Oxygen In-take," *The Physician and Sports Medicine*, 5, no. 7 (July 1977): p. 55.

8. Cummings, Elsie J. and Charlton, Wavie J., *Survival: Pioneer, Indian and Wilderness Lore* (St. Ignatius, Montana: Mission Valley News, 1971), p. 33.

9. Leavy, Jane, "Is Our New Lifestyle Changing our Menstrual Cycle?" *Self*, January 1979, pp. 91–93.

10. Ibid.

11. Physicians' Desk Reference. (Oradell, New Jersey: Litton Industries, 1978), Supplements A and B.

12. Wilkerson, op. cit., pp. 203–206.
13. Ibid.
14. Ibid., p. 261.
15. Hackett, Peter H. and Drummond, Rennie, "Rales, Peripheral Edema, Retinal Hemmorrhage and Acute Mountain Sickness," *American Journal of Medicine*, 67 (1979):214–218.
16. Wilkerson, op. cit., pp. 246–247.
17. Lindsay, Rae, *How to Look as Young as You Feel* (Century City, California: Pinnacle Books, 1980), p. 77.
18. Hackett, op. cit., pp. 214–218.
19. Hackett, Peter H. and Drummond, Rennie, "Acute Mountain Sickness," *Lancet*, 1 (1977):491.
20. Leavy, Jane, "Is the Exercise That's Good for You Good for the Baby?" *Self*, August 1979, pp. 84–87.
21. Abelson, Andrew E., "Altitude and Fertility," *Human Biology*, 48 (1976) pp. 83–92.
Eckes, L. and McClung, J., "Effects of High Altitude on Human Birth" (Cambridge: Harvard University Press, 1979).
22. Leavy, op. cit.
23. Brewer, V. and Hinson, M., "Relationship of Pregnancy to Lateral Knee Stability," *Medicine and Science in Sports*, no. 10 (1978):39.

Chapter Six
Perils and Precautions

1. U. S. Forest Service, Department of Agriculture, *Snow Avalanche* (Missoula, Montana, 1971).
2. Hackett, Peter H.; Drummond, Rennie; and Levine, H. D., "The Incidence, Importance and Prophylaxis of Acute Mountain Sickness," Lancet 2 (1976):1150.
Wilkerson, op. cit., pp. 140–142.
Wilkerson, op. cit., p. 321.
3. Wilkerson, op. cit., p. 156.
4. U.S. Forest Service, Department of Agriculture, *Heat Stress* (Missoula, Montana: U.S. Government Printing Office: 1979):699–953.
5. Shibolet, S.; Lancaster, M.C.; and Danon, Y., "Heat Stroke: A Review," *Aviation, Space, and Environmental Medicine*, 47:280–301.
6. Dr. Sarah A. Nunneley, United States Air Force School of Aerospace Medicine, Brooks Air Force Base, Texas: Personal correspondence with authors, 1980.
7. Ibid.
8. Craighead, John J. and Frank C. Jr., "Grizzly Bear-Man Relationships in Yellowstone National Park," *Bioscience*, 21 (1971):845–857.
9. Murie, Olaus J., *A Field Guide to Animal Tracks* (2d ed. Boston: Houghton Mifflin Co., 1974).

10. Herrero, Stephen, "Human Injury Inflicted by Grizzly Bears," *Science*, 170 (1970):593–598.

11. Jonkel, Charles J., "Of Bears and People," *Western Wildlands*, 2 (1975):33.

12. Schneider, Bill, *Where the Grizzly Walks* (Missoula, Montana: Mountain Press Publishing Co., 1977), pp. 72–76.

13. "Halt," manufactured by Animal Repellents, Inc., Griffin, Georgia 30223.

14. Dean, Frederick C., program leader, University of Alaska, Alaska Cooperative Park Studies Unit; Memorandum concerning fifth International Conference on Bear Biology and Management, February 1980.

15. Brownmiller, Susan, *Against Our Will: Men, Women and Rape* (New York: Simon and Schuster, 1975), pp. 183–186.

16. Ibid., p. 176.

17. Ibid., p. 182.

References

Chapter Three
Physical Fitness

American College of Sports Medicine Opinion Statement. "The Participation of the Female Athlete in Long-Distance Running." *Medicine and Science in Sports*, 11 (1979).

Dale, Edwin. "Physical Fitness Profiles and Reproductive Physiology of the Female Distance Runner." *The Physician and Sports Medicine*, 7 (1979):83–95.

Folinsbee, Lawrence. *Environmental Stress: Individual Human Adaptations*. New York: Academic Press, 1978.

Kaplan, Janice. *Women and Sports*. New York: Viking Press, 1979.

Lance, Kathryn *Getting Strong*. New York: Bobbs-Merrill Co., 1978.

Miller, Benjamin F., M.D. *The Complete Medical Guide*. 3d ed. New York: Simon and Schuster, 1967.

"Playing While Pregnant." *Ms.*, July 1978, p. 48.

"Pregnancy." *Encyclopedia Britannica*, 15th ed. 1976, pp. 968–983.

"Sperm." *Encyclopedia Britannica*, 15th ed. 1976, p. 414.

Chapter Four
Great Expectations

American Red Cross. *First Aid.* 4th ed. New York: Doubleday and Co.., 1970.
Early Winters, 1980 Catalogue, 110 Prefontaine Place South, Seattle, Washington.
Eastern Mountain Sports, 1980 Spring/Summer and Fall/Winter catalogues, Vose Farm Road, Peterborough, New Hampshire, 03458.
Holubar Mountaineering Ltd., 1979/80 catalogues, Box 7, Boulder, Colorado, 80306.
Official Boy Scout Handbook. 9th ed. New Brunswick, New Jersey, Boy Scouts of America, 1979.
The Co-op catalogues, Recreational Equipment Co., 1979, Box C–88125, Seattle, Washington, 98188.
The 1980 Ski Hut catalogues, Box 309, Berkely, California, 94701.
Sierra Designs, 1980 catalogues, 247 Fourth St., Oakland, CA 94607.
Winnett, Thomas. *Backpacking in the Wilderness Rockies.* New York: Ballantine Books, 1973.

Chapter Five
Fail Safe for the Better Half

Angier, Bradford, *How to Stay Alive in the Woods.* Ontario, Canada: Collier-MacMillan Books, 1958.
Speak, P. and Carter, A.H.C. *Map Reading and Interpretation.* London, England: Longman Group, 1964.
Putnam, William C. *Map Interpretation with Military Application.* New York: McGraw-Hill Co., 1943.

Chapter Six
Perils and Precautions

Cole, Glen F. "Management Involving Grizzly Bears and Humans in Yellowstone National Park, 1970–1973." *Bioscience,* 24 (1974): 335–338.
Cushing, Bruce S. "The Effects of Human Menstruation on the Polar Bear." Mimeographed. Missoula, Montana: University of Montana, 1979.
Olsen, Jack. *Night of the Grizzlies.* New York: G. P. Putnam and Sons, 1969.
U.S. Forest Service. *The Snowy Torrents: Avalanche Accidents in the United States: 1967–1971.* Fort Collins, Colorado: Rocky Mountain Forest and Range Experiment Station. General Technical Report RM–8, March 1975.
U.S. Forest Service. *Winter Recreation Safety Guide.* Government Printing Program, Program Aid No. 1140, Stock No. 001–000–03577–1.

Index